Prologue

I emigrated from Korea to America 36 years ago. Away from my family and home for the first time in my life, I was miserable. America (or at least Chicago, where my husband and I had settled) was enormous, intimidating, and so very foreign. Two weeks into my new life in the United States, I received a much needed call from my mother. She patiently bore my tears and complaints and then asked me to gather a few things from the refrigerator. Food? How could I think of food when my world had been turned upside down? Over the next half hour or so, my mother directed me as I prepared my favorite meal, a spicy cabbage stew. Like Proust's madeleine, the taste of my mother's cabbage stew instantly evoked warm memories of home and family. All was right with the world once again.

Fast forward 30 years (and hundreds of memory creating meals prepared for my husband and two sons). I am a student at Kendall College's School of Culinary Arts in Chicago. Although I had received culinary training in Korea at the Institute of Korean Royal Cuisine, I wanted professional exposure to western cooking styles and techniques. As a culinary student, I learned the ins and outs of various western cuisines and began to apply these lessons to the Korean fare I had been preparing for years. I wanted to maintain the integrity of traditional Korean cooking (too many "fusion" efforts come from a fundamental misunderstanding of Korean cuisine). At the same time, I sensed that certain western ingredients and techniques could complement and enhance even the most basic of Korean staples.

As it happens, my daughter-in-law, a Korean native who had also received culinary training in the United States, had begun a similar project. I still remember first speaking to my daughter-in-law about these concepts. A casual dinnertime conversation evolved into a four hour discourse on food and cooking. We spent the next few years reifying our ideas, seeking to harmonize the elements of eastern and western culinary sensibilities.

This book is the fruit of those labors. The recipes that follow do not represent a radical departure from traditional Korean cooking. Rather, we carefully chose our spots, synthesizing styles only where we thought a genuine contribution could be made. In some instances, we present recipes that have been passed down unchanged over several generations. For our Korean readers, we hope these recipes will bring back memories of hearth and home while introducing an element of mystery and adventure. For our non-Korean readers, we hope to bring a degree of accessibility to a cuisine that many consider unfamiliar and exotic. For all, we hope this book helps you create delicious meals that will provide comfort and happiness for you and those you love.

We could not have completed this book without the help and encouragement of so many. Special thanks go to David, Dan, and Lise Yoo, Terry Lim, Rugalta Kim, Young Shim Lee, Hellen Kim, Kee Joo Hong, Jung Soo Han, Mee Soon Bae, Jean Hee Lee, my church pastors and members, the Rotary One members and friends who took the time to write the congratulatory notes, everyone at the Chicago Joong-Ang Daily and Wind Magazine, and my loving husband Chang.

'요리는 예술이요 사랑이자 기쁨의 나눔' 입니다.

36년 전! 대학을 마치고 좀 더 많은 것을 배우고자 사랑하는 가족과 집을 떠나 유학생 남편을 따라 낯선 시카고 땅에 정착했습니다. 외로운 나의 마음을 전화로 달래주시던 엄마의 목소리… 엄마의 제안으로 내가 제일 좋아하는 김치찌개를 만들어 보며, 엄마가 해주던 음식을 만들어 가면서 가족을 그리워하는 마음을 달래고 따뜻한 추억을 만들어 가게 되었습니다.

30여 년이라는 세월은 빨리 지나갔습니다. 지금은 변호사가 된 큰아들, 회사 CFO가 된 작은아들을 다 키워 보내고 빈 둥지만 바라보던 나는 다시 학교로 돌아가 젊어서 못한 미술 공부를 요리에 접목시켜 한식을 세계화하는 데 일조를 해보자는 작은 소망을 갖게 되었습니다. 요리대학에서 공부하면서 외국음식에 대한 지식을 쌓고, 한국에 나가 궁중요리를 배워 그것을 기초로 현지 재료와 외국요리를 접목하여 한국음식을 멋지게 프레젠테이션 하여 책을 만들어 보자는 생각에 이르러 몇 년 동안 준비를 하게 되었습니다.

다행히도 한국에서 자란 큰며느리 정화가 요리에 관심이 많고 그동안 많은 쿠킹 클래스를 이수하여, 며느리와 만나면 늘 음식에 대한 이야기로 꽃을 피웠습니다. 며느리와 나는 서로 아이디어를 내어 한국요리를 동서양요리에 접목하여 세계화 시킬 수 있는 책을 만들어 보자는 데에 마음의 일치가 되었고, 3년에 걸쳐 요리책에 관련된 구체적인 노력을 기울인 결과 이 책을 출간하게 되었습니다.

이 책은 한국 전통음식 그대로의 레서피가 아니라 한국인에게는 한국음식을 이렇게 퓨전화 시킬 수 있다는 것을 알리고, 외국인들에게는 잘 몰랐던 색다른 한국음식을 쉽게 접근할 수 있도록 현지 재료 등을 사용하여 레서피를 만들었습니다.

그리하여 이 책으로 만들어진 맛있는 한국음식이 세계인들에게 행복과 건강을 줄 수 있기를 바라는 마음입니다.

부족한 저에게 과찬의 축하글을 보내주신 로터리 원 멤버와 한인 여러분들께 감사의 말씀 드립니다. 특별히 늘 옆에서 조언해 주신 배미순 원장님, 푸드칼럼을 내주신 중앙일보와 윈드 잡지 관계자분들, 던디마켓 직원님들, 그릇을 협찬해 주신 하이마트 직원님들, 사진작가 한정수 실장님, 푸드스타일리스트 홍기주 님, 루갈타 김 님, 이영심 님, 김정순 님, 큰며느리 정화, 큰아들 데이빗, 작은아들 며느리 댄과 리스, 테리, 용기를 북돋아 준 가까운 나의 친구들 그리고 리스컴 출판사 이진희 사장님과 편집자들께 감사드립니다. 교회 일에 소홀했음에도 지켜봐주신 목사님들과 교우분들께 감사드립니다. 무엇보다도 1년 내내 음식 맛 봐주고 건강 보살펴주느라 수고하신 남편(유창성)에게 사랑과 고마움을 보내며 이 모든 영광을 하나님께 드립니다.

저자 유소연

Korean Culinary Traditions
Special Food Preparations for Special Occasions

특별한 날, 특별한 상차림

Food figures prominently in Korean holidays and celebrations. The two most important Korean holidays, New Year's Day and Thanksgiving, are observed through the preparation of specific types of food. Special food preparations are also involved in a child's first birthday, perhaps the most joyous of Korean celebrations.

한국에는 특별한 날 특별히 준비하는 음식들이 있습니다. 새해 첫날에는 멥쌀로 가래떡을 뽑아 떡국을 끓이고, 추석에는 햇곡식으로 송편을 빚어 먹습니다. 혼례상이나 첫돌을 맞은 아기의 생일상도 특별한 의미를 담고 있습니다. 그밖에도 한국에는 절기마다 그 계절에 나는 신선한 재료로 음식을 만들어 나누어 먹는 전통이 있습니다.

New Year's Day
설날상차림

The first day of the New Year (based on the lunar Korean calendar) is called Seolnal in Korean. Seolnal is considered the most important of the Korean holidays. Koreans celebrate Seolnal by gathering with family members to enjoy a meal, play traditional Korean games such as yutnori, and pay their respects to their elders. Koreans honor their elders on this day through a practice called Saebae. This practice involves the donning of traditional Korean garb, called han-bok, and the performing of a ceremonial bow to parents and older family members.

The Seolnal meal traditionally consists of a rice cake soup, pan-fried fish, and a noodle dish called jabchae. The rice cake soup is made using long sticks of rice cake that are cut diagonally into thin slices. The preparation of the rice cake symbolizes both a long life and a clean start. The Seolnal meal is then finished off with a sweet rice drink (shikhye) and a fruit punch (soojung-gua).

새해 첫 날을 '설날' 이라고 하여, 아침 일찍 일어나 새 옷으로 갈아입고 조상들께 차례를 지냅니다. 돌아가신 조상들께 차례를 지내고 나면 살아계신 부모님이나 웃어른들께 세배를 하고 온가족이 둘러앉아 음식을 나누어 먹습니다.
설날 상차림에는 떡국 또는 떡만두국이 주 메뉴로 오르며, 그밖에 산적, 전유어, 잡채 등의 음식이 상에 오릅니다. 떡국은 길게 뽑은 가래떡을 어슷하게 썰어서 만드는데, 이 기다란 가래떡은 건강하게 오래 살라는 의미와 한 해를 깨끗한 마음으로 시작하자는 의미가 담겨 있습니다. 떡국과 고기, 전, 나물 등으로 식사를 마치고 나면 식혜나 수정과, 약식이나 강정으로 다과상을 차립니다.

Thanksgiving
추석상차림

On August 15th of each year (based on the Korean lunar calendar), Koreans give thanks to their ancestors for a successful harvest. Korean society is no longer primarily agricultural, but the tradition and general sentiment remain. As with most Korean holidays and celebrations, Thanksgiving is observed through a family meal. The Thanksgiving meal is best known for its rice cakes (song-pyun), stuffed with red bean paste, sesame seeds, and crushed chestnuts. These rice cakes, once stuffed, are steamed on a layer of pine needles. The Thanksgiving meal also features taro soup, beef jerky, various fruits, chestnuts, and dates. The variety of the meal represents the bounty for which Korean families give thanks each year.

서양의 추수감사절에 해당하는 추석은 설과 함께 가장 큰 명절로 꼽힙니다. 음력으로 8월 15일, 양력으로는 9월말에서 10월초에 해당하며, 추수가 한창인 시기라서 곡식과 과일이 풍부합니다. 이런 풍성한 햇과일과 햇곡식으로 조상들께 한 해 농사를 감사하는 제사를 지냅니다.

추석상의 주 메뉴는 햅쌀로 빚은 송편이며, 가을 제철을 맞은 토란으로 곰탕을 끓여 송편과 함께 올립니다. 송편은 햅쌀을 빻아 반죽한 다음, 속에 거피팥이나 콩, 참깨, 으깬 밤 등으로 달콤한 소를 만들어 넣고 반달 모양으로 빚어 찐 떡입니다. 솔잎을 깔고 쪄서 솔잎 향이 나기 때문에 '송편' 이라는 이름이 붙었습니다. 송편과 토란탕 외에 포와 적, 색색의 햇과일과 밤, 대추 등으로 풍성하고도 화려한 한상을 차립니다.

The First Birthday
돌상차림

A child's first birthday, or dohl, has special meaning in Korean culture because Korean children in the past often did not survive their first birthday. Although modern medicine has brought improvements over the last few decades, the arrival of a child's first birthday still represents a joyous occasion. Korean families celebrate a child's dohl by dressing the child in traditional Korean garb and placing the child on a large mat that contains several objects. Each of these objects, which may vary from dohl to dohl, symbolizes a specific fortune for the child. For example, a bowl of rice symbolizes prosperity, a pencil symbolizes a life of scholarship, and a ball of yarn represents longevity. The first object that the child grabs is said to represent the child's path in life.

To mark the importance of this celebration, families prepare foods that symbolize long life, health, and good fortune. These foods include fruits, dates, rice cakes, and a seaweed soup with noodles. Often, these foods will be stacked on a table and used as decoration for the celebration.

생일상차림 중에서도 태어난 지 100일이 되는 날에 차리는 백일상과, 태어나 1년을 맞이하는 날 차리는 돌상은 특별한 의미를 지닙니다. 의학이 발달하지 않은 과거에는 태어나서 1년을 넘기지 못하는 아이가 많았다고 합니다. 그래서 1년 맞이하는 생일을 축하하며 앞으로의 무병장수를 비는 의미에서 특별한 상을 차렸습니다.

돌상은 순수하고 건강하게 자라라는 의미에서 백설기와 수수경단, 미역국, 흰밥으로 차리고 국수를 올리기도 합니다. 그밖에 대추와 과일을 상에 올립니다.

Contents

Appetizers 애피타이저

Salads 샐러드

Meats & Seafood 고기와 해산물

Beef

Pork

Poultry

Seafood

Soups & Stews 국과 찌개

Rice Dishes 밥

Noodles & Rice Cakes 국수와 떡볶이

Sides 반찬

Desserts 디저트

Etc.

We love making these appetizers because they can be prepared to please both the palate and the eye. Appetizers lend themselves to creative presentations, and of course the best meals appeal to all of our senses.

전채요리를 만드는 것은 며느리와 내가 아주 즐겨하는 일이랍니다.
맛과 멋의 조화를 한껏 낼 수 있기 때문이지요. 보기에 예쁜 음식은 먹는 데도 즐거움이 있답니다.

Appetizers

애피타이저

Jeon in Three Acts - Zucchini, Ground Beef, Cod 삼색전

Stuffed Anaheim Peppers 고추전

Seafood Jeon Haemul Pajeon 해물파전

Mung Bean Jeon Nokdu Jeon 녹두전

Korean-Style Vermicelli Jabchae 잡채

Fried Crab Dumplings 게살 튀김만두

Finger Eggroll 핑거 에그롤

Fried Dumplings Twigim Mandu 튀김만두

Pork and Chive Dumplings 돼지고기 부추만두

Spring Roll 스프링 롤

Shrimp and Crab Meat Stuffed Avocado 새우와 게살이 들어간 아보카도

Tofu Stuffed Baked Clams 대합구이

Grilled King Oyster Mushroom Skewers 새송이 꼬치

Oyster Shot 굴회

Korean Beef Tartare Yook Hwae 육회

4 Servings

Zucchini Jeon

1 (12 oz.)	Korean zucchini, cut into 1/4-inch thick slices
TT*	Salt

Ground Beef Jeon

4 oz.	Beef, ground
4 oz.	Firm tofu, squeezed
3 Tbsp	Scallion, chopped
1/2 Tbsp	Garlic, minced
2 tsp	Sesame oil
1 Tbsp	Sesame seeds
TT*	Salt, pepper

Cod Jeon

10 oz.	Cod, cut into 1/4-inch thick pieces
TT*	Salt, pepper

3	Eggs, whipped (egg wash)
1 cup	Flour
As needed	Vegetable oil

*TT : To Taste

Preparation

1 Season zucchini with salt. Dredge pieces of zucchini in flour, shake off excess, and dip in egg wash. Heat vegetable oil in a large pan over medium heat and cook both sides of zucchini until lightly browned.

2 Mix ground beef, tofu, scallions, garlic, sesame oil, sesame seeds, salt, and pepper. Form mixture into balls and flatten to desired thickness. Dredge in flour, shake off excess, and dip in egg wash. Heat oil in a large pan over medium heat and cook both sides until lightly browned.

3 Season cod slices with salt and pepper. Dredge cod in flour, shake off excess, and dip in egg wash. Heat oil in a large pan over medium heat and cook both sides of cod until lightly browned.

4 Serve with dipping sauce.

Tip [1] To make dipping sauce, combine 1 tablespoon soy sauce, 1/2 tablespoon vinegar, 1 teaspoon lemon, 1/2 teaspoon sugar and 1 teaspoon sesame seeds.

[2] Any kind of zucchini can be substituted for Korean zucchini.

4 인분

호박전
애호박 (0.5cm 두께로) 1개, 소금 적당량

고기전
갈은 쇠고기 115 g, 꼭 짠 부침용 두부 115 g, 다진 파 3 큰술, 다진 마늘 1/2 큰술, 참기름 2 작은술, 참깨 1 큰술, 소금 · 후추 적당량

대구전
0.5cm 두께로 썬 대구 300 g, 소금 · 후추 적당량

달걀 3 개, 밀가루 1 컵, 식용유 적당량

준비 과정

1 호박은 소금으로 간을 한 후 밀가루를 묻혀 털어내고, 달걀 푼 물에 적십니다. 식용유를 두른 중불 프라이팬에 앞뒤로 지져냅니다.

2 갈은 쇠고기와 물기를 짠 두부에 파, 마늘, 참기름, 참깨, 소금과 후추를 넣고 잘 섞은 후 둥글납작하게 모양을 만들어 놓습니다. 밀가루에 묻혀 털어낸 후 달걀물에 적셔 식용유를 두른 프라이팬에 고기가 익을 때까지 앞뒤로 지져냅니다.

3 대구살은 소금과 후추로 밑간을 합니다. 밀가루를 묻혀 털어내고, 달걀 푼 물에 밀가루 부분이 고루 적셔지도록 담갔다 식용유를 두른 중불 프라이팬에 앞뒤로 지져냅니다.

4 세 가지 전을 찍어 먹는 소스와 함께 상에 냅니다.

Tip [1] 간장 1큰술, 식초 1/2큰술, 레몬즙 1 작은술, 설탕1/2 작은술, 참깨 1 작은술을 섞어 찍어 드시면 좋습니다.

[2] 애호박이 없으면 다른 호박으로 대체하셔도 됩니다.

Stuffed Anaheim Peppers
고추전

4 Servings

4	Anaheim peppers
1/2 lb.	Beef, ground
4 oz.	Tofu, squeezed
1 cup	Flour
2	Eggs, whipped (egg wash)
As needed	Vegetable oil

Seasoning

2 Tbsp	Scallion, chopped
1/2 Tbsp	Garlic, minced
1 tsp	Sesame oil
1 Tbsp	Sesame seeds
TT*	Salt, pepper

Dipping Sauce

2 Tbsp	Soy sauce
2 Tbsp	Lemon juice
1 Tbsp	Dijon mustard
1 tsp	Sugar
1 tsp	Scallion, chopped
TT*	Salt, pepper

*TT : To Taste

Preparation

1 Combine dipping sauce ingredients in a small bowl. Set aside.

2 Slice Anaheim peppers in half lengthwise and remove seeds. Rinse and blot dry with paper towel.

3 Combine ground beef, tofu, and seasoning ingredients in a large bowl. Lightly dredge peppers in flour and shake off excess. Overstuff each half pepper with the ground beef and tofu mixture.

4 Dredge stuffed peppers in flour, dip in egg wash, and shake off excess.

5 Heat vegetable oil in a large pan over medium-high heat. Add peppers (stuffing side down) and cook for 7~8 minutes. Turn peppers over and cook for an additional 3~4 minutes.

6 Serve peppers with dipping sauce.

Tip For a deeper char, grill stuffed peppers for 2~3 minutes (pepper side down) after pan frying.

4 인분

4개	애너하임고추(또는 풋고추)
225 g	갈은 쇠고기
115 g	물기를 꼭 짠 두부
1 컵	밀가루
2개	달걀
적당량	식용유

양념
다진 파 2 큰술, 다진 마늘 1 큰술, 참기름 1 작은술, 참깨 1큰술, 소금 · 후추 적당량

찍어 먹는 소스
간장 2 큰술, 레몬즙 2 큰술, 디존 머스터드 1 큰술, 설탕 1 작은술, 다진 파 1 작은술, 소금 · 후추 적당량

준비 과정

1 찍어 먹는 소스 재료를 한데 섞어둡니다.

2 고추를 세로로 반 잘라 씨를 빼내고, 속살을 깨끗이 씻어서 물기가 없게 닦아 준비해 놓습니다.

3 고기와 두부를 양념에 잘 섞은 후 물기가 마른 고추 속에 밀가루를 살짝 묻힌 다음 고추 위로 살짝 올라올 만큼 고기 속을 채워 넣습니다.

4 속을 채운 고추에 밀가루를 고루 묻힌 다음 달걀물에 적십니다.

5 중불 프라이팬에 식용유를 두르고 고기 부분을 먼저 7~8분 구워낸 다음 뒤집어서 3~4분 정도 더 구워 줍니다.

6 고추전을 찍어 먹는 소스와 함께 상에 냅니다.

Tip 다 구워진 고추전을 그릴 위에 올려 2~3분 살짝 한 번 더 구워내면 훨씬 맛있습니다.

Seafood Jeon Haemul Pajeon
해물파전

4 Servings

5 oz.	Shrimp, chopped
5 oz.	Crab sticks, chopped
5 oz.	Squid, chopped
3 stalks	Scallion, chopped
As needed	Vegetable oil

Batter

1/4 cup	Flour
1/3 cup	Water
1	Egg
1 Tbsp	Onion powder
1 Tbsp	Garlic powder
1 tsp	Sugar
TT*	Salt, pepper

Dipping Sauce

1 Tbsp	Soy sauce
1/2 Tbsp	Vinegar
1 tsp	Lemon juice
1/2 tsp	Brown sugar
1 tsp	Sesame seeds
1 Tbsp	Scallion, chopped

*TT : To Taste

Preparation

1 Combine dipping sauce ingredients in a small bowl. Set aside.

2 Combine water, flour, and egg to make a batter (pancake batter consistency).

3 Add onion powder, garlic powder, sugar, salt, pepper, chopped shrimp, crab meat, squid, and scallion to the batter.

4 Heat vegetable oil in a large pan over medium-high heat. Place large spoonfuls of batter in the pan. Each jeon should be round and not thicker than 1/3 of an inch. Cook both sides of each jeon until golden brown.

5 Serve seafood jeon with dipping sauce.

Tip Most Asian markets sell pre-made jeon mix.

---

4 인분

140 g	다진 새우
140 g	다진 게살
140 g	다진 오징어
3 줄기	다진 파
적당량	식용유

반죽

밀가루 1/4 컵, 물 1/3 컵, 달걀 1 개, 양파가루 1 큰술,
마늘가루 1 큰술, 설탕 1 작은술, 소금 · 후추 적당량

찍어 먹는 소스

간장 1 큰술, 식초 1/2 큰술, 레몬즙 1 작은술,
흑설탕 1/2 작은술, 참깨 1 작은술, 다진 파 1 큰술

준비 과정

1 찍어 먹는 소스 재료를 볼에 넣어 한데 섞어둡니다.

2 밀가루에 물과 달걀을 넣어 팬케이크 반죽 정도의 묽기로 반죽을 만듭니다.

3 반죽에 분량의 양파가루, 마늘가루, 설탕, 소금, 후추, 다진 새우, 게살, 오징어, 파를 넣고 섞어 줍니다.

4 중불 프라이팬에 식용유를 두르고 재료를 큰 수저로 떠서 동그랗고 얇게 펴줍니다. 전 두께가 1cm 이상 되지 않도록 펴주면서 양쪽이 모두 노릇하고 바삭하도록 익혀줍니다.

5 전을 꺼내 찍어 먹는 소스와 함께 상에 냅니다.

Tip 반죽 대신 한국 마켓에서 부침가루를 사다 쓰면 편리합니다. 부침가루를 쓰면 반죽에 들어가는 양념은 넣지 않습니다.

Mung Bean Jeon Nokdu Jeon
녹두전

4~6 Servings

1 cup	Mung beans
1/3	Onion, chopped fine
8 oz.	Pork belly, chopped
8 oz.	Green bean sprouts
1 cup	Ripe kimchi, chopped
3 stalks	Scallion, chopped
1/2 tsp	Salt
TT*	Pepper
As needed	Vegetable oil

Seasoning

1 Tbsp	Soy sauce
1 tsp	Sugar
1 tsp	Garlic, minced
1/2 tsp	Ginger, minced
1 tsp	Sesame oil

Dipping Sauce

1 Tbsp	Soy sauce
1/2 Tbsp	Vinegar
1 tsp	Sugar
1 tsp	Lemon juice
TT*	Pepper

*TT : To Taste

Preparation

1 Combine dipping sauce ingredients in a small bowl. Set aside.

2 Rinse mung beans and soak in water for 3 hours. Remove and place beans and onions in a blender. While blending, slowly add water until mixture is thick and uniform in consistency.

3 Combine pork belly with seasoning ingredients in a large bowl.

4 Blanch green bean sprouts and squeeze out excess water. Cut into bite-sized pieces.

5 Combine chopped pork belly and green bean sprouts with kimchi, chopped scallion, and salt in a large bowl. Let sit for a few minutes and pour in bean blend. Mix well.

6 Heat vegetable oil in a large pan over medium heat. Place large spoonfuls of mixture in the pan. Each jeon should be round and not thicker than 1/3 of an inch. Cook both sides of each jeon until golden brown.

7 Serve mung bean jeon with dipping sauce.

Tip Add more or less salt depending on the salt content of the kimchi.

4~6 인분

1 컵	녹두
1/3 개분	잘게 다진 양파
220 g	잘게 다진 돼지고기 삼겹살
220 g	숙주
1 컵	다진 익은 김치
3 줄기	다진 파
1/2 작은술	소금
적당량	식용유
적당량	후추

돼지고기 삼겹살 양념
간장 1 큰술, 설탕 1 작은술, 다진 마늘 1 작은술,
다진 생강 1/2 작은술, 참기름 1 작은술

찍어 먹는 소스
간장 1 큰술, 식초 1 큰술, 설탕 1 작은술,
레몬즙 1 작은술, 후추 적당량

준비 과정

1 찍어 먹는 소스 재료를 한데 섞어 준비합니다.

2 녹두를 깨끗이 씻어 3시간 정도 물에 불립니다. 물을 따라내고 다진 양파와 불린 녹두를 블렌더에 넣고 물을 넣어가며 곱고 되직하게 갈아줍니다.

3 다진 돼지고기 삼겹살은 양념에 버무려 놓습니다.

4 숙주나물은 뜨거운 물에 살짝 데쳐서 찬물에 넣었다 물기를 꼭 짜서 먹기 좋게 썰어둡니다.

5 돼지고기 삼겹살과 숙주나물에 익은 김치, 다진 파, 소금을 넣어 버무린 후 갈은 녹두에 함께 섞어줍니다.

6 중불 프라이팬에 식용유를 두르고 숟가락으로 크게 재료를 떠서 1cm 두께가 넘지 않도록 동그랗고 납작하게 모양을 잡아줍니다. 앞뒤로 속 재료가 다 익을 때까지 노릇노릇하고 바삭하게 부쳐줍니다.

7 녹두전이 뜨거울 때 찍어 먹는 소스와 함께 드시면 좋습니다.

Tip 김치 맛에 따라 간이 다르므로 소금 양을 조절해 줍니다.

Mung beans 녹두

Korean-Style Vermicelli Jabchae
잡채

4~6 Servings

6 oz.	Sweet potato starch noodles
3 oz.	Beef sirloin, sliced thin
1/3	Carrot, julienned
1	Onion, medium-sized, julienned
7~8	Shitake mushrooms, sliced thin
1	Kirby cucumber, julienned
2	Eggs, cooked into omelet and sliced thin
As needed	Sesame oil
As needed	Olive oil
TT*	Soy sauce, sesame oil, sugar, salt

Seasoning

4 Tbsp	Soy sauce
1/2 Tbsp	Garlic, minced
1/2 Tbsp	Scallion, chopped
1 Tbsp	Sesame oil
1 Tbsp	Sesame seeds
1 $\frac{1}{2}$ Tbsp	Sugar

*TT : To Taste

Preparation

1 Combine seasoning ingredients in a small bowl. Set aside.

2 Bring water and a pinch of salt to a boil in a medium pot. Add noodles and cook for 5~7 minutes or until soft. Rinse noodles in cold water and drain completely. Place noodles in a large bowl and mix with 1 tablespoon each of olive and sesame oil. Set aside.

3 Place cucumbers in a small bowl and add a pinch of salt. Let sit for about 30 minutes and carefully squeeze out excess liquid.

4 Sauté beef with 1 tablespoon of seasoning mixture in a large pan over medium-high heat. In 2~3 minute intervals, add carrots and onions, shitake mushrooms, and cucumbers (in that order).

5 Mix together beef, vegetables, and mushrooms with the noodles. Add sugar, soy sauce, and sesame oil to taste.

6 Serve jabchae garnished with egg omelet slices.

4~6 인분

170 g	당면
85 g	얇게 썬 쇠고기
1/3 개분	채 썬 당근
1 개분	채 썬 양파
7-8 개분	채 썬 표고버섯
1 개분	채 썬 오이
2 개분	달걀지단
적당량	참기름
적당량	올리브오일
적당량	간장, 참기름, 설탕, 소금

양념
간장 4 큰술, 다진 마늘 1/2 큰술, 다진 파 1/2 큰술,
참기름 1 큰술, 참깨 1 큰술, 설탕 1 $\frac{1}{2}$ 큰술

준비 과정

1 양념 소스 재료를 한데 섞어둡니다

2 당면은 끓는 물에 소금을 넣고 부드러워질 때까지 5~7분 끓여 찬물에 헹궈 물기를 뺀 후 올리브오일 1큰술, 참기름 1큰술을 넣고 버무려 놓습니다.

3 작은 볼에 오이를 넣고 소금을 살짝 뿌려 30분 정도 둔 후 물기를 꼭 짜놓습니다.

4 중불 프라이팬에 올리브오일을 두르고, 쇠고기와 양념 1큰술을 넣고 볶습니다. 2~3분 간격으로 먼저 당근과 양파를 넣고 볶다가, 표고버섯을 넣고, 그 다음 오이를 넣어 볶아줍니다. 야채와 버섯을 볶을 때 양념 1큰술씩을 더 넣고 볶습니다.

5 큰 볼에 당면국수와 모든 재료를 넣고 한데 섞어 버무립니다. 기호에 따라 설탕, 간장, 참기름을 마지막 버무릴 때 더 넣어도 좋습니다.

6 잡채를 담고 달걀지단을 올려 상에 냅니다.

Tip 야채와 고기를 따로 따로 볶아 섞어주면 더욱 좋습니다.

Sweet potato starch noodles 당면

Fried Crab Dumplings

게살 튀김만두

4 Servings (16 pieces)

4	Spring roll wrappers, cut into quarters
6 oz.	Shrimp, cut into 1/2-inch long pieces
6 oz.	Crab sticks, cut into 1/2-inch long pieces
6 Tbsp	Plain cream cheese
1	Egg, whipped (egg wash)
As needed	Canola oil

Dipping Sauce

7 Tbsp	Sweet and sour sauce
1½ Tbsp	Lemon juice
2 Tbsp	Parsley, chopped
1/2 Tbsp	Sugar
TT *	Pepper

*TT : To Taste

Preparation

1 Combine dipping sauce ingredients in a small bowl. Set aside.

2 Brush the edges of a spring roll wrapper with egg wash (you can do this with your finger). Place one or two pieces of shrimp, one piece of crab, and 1 teaspoon of cream cheese in the center of the wrapper. Pinch the centers of each wrapper's edge together and seal the edges well.

3 Fill a wok or medium-sized pot halfway up with canola oil and bring to 350°F. Add dumplings and deep-fry until golden brown and crispy. Remove dumplings and place on paper towel to allow excess oil to drain.

4 Serve dumplings with dipping sauce.

4 인분 (16개)

4 장	4조각으로 자른 라이스 페이퍼
170 g	1cm로 썬 새우
170 g	1cm로 썬 게맛살
6 큰술	플레인 크림치즈
1 개분	달걀물
적당량	카놀라 오일

찍어 먹는 소스
스윗 앤 사워 소스 7 큰술, 레몬즙 1 ½ 큰술,
다진 파슬리 2 큰술, 설탕 1/2 큰술, 후추 적당량

준비 과정

1 찍어 먹는 소스 재료를 한데 섞어둡니다.

2 달걀물을 풀어 자른 라이스 페이퍼 가장자리에 바르고 자른 새우 한두 개와 게살을 하나씩 올린 후 크림치즈 1작은술 정도를 넣습니다. 더 바삭한 만두 질감을 내기 위해서 라이스 페이퍼 가장자리 가운데 네 부분을 잡아 중간으로 올린 후 가장자리 부분을 잘 여며 줍니다. 그러면 네 귀퉁이가 생긴 만두 모양이 나옵니다.

3 175℃ 기름에 튀긴 후 기름이 빠지도록 종이타월 위에 둡니다.

4 찍어 먹는 소스를 곁들여 상에 냅니다.

Finger Eggroll
핑거 에그롤

4 Servings

6 oz.	Shrimp, ground
6 oz.	Pork, ground
3 Tbsp	Parsley, chopped
3 Tbsp	Shallot, minced
3 Tbsp	Peanut butter
1/2 tsp	Salt
TT*	Pepper
6	Spring roll wrappers, cut into halves
1	Egg, whipped (egg wash)
As needed	Canola oil

Dipping Sauce

7 Tbsp	Sweet and sour sauce
1½ Tbsp	Lemon juice
2 Tbsp	Parsley, chopped
1/2 Tbsp	Sugar
TT*	Pepper

*TT : To Taste

Preparation

1 Combine dipping sauce ingredients in a small bowl. Set aside.

2 Combine shrimp, pork, parsley, shallot, peanut butter, salt, and pepper in a large bowl.

3 Brush the edges of a spring roll wrapper with egg wash (you can do this with your finger). Place filling mixture down the middle of the wrapper. Roll the wrapper around the filling and fold the two outer ends toward the middle. Continue rolling the wrapper and seal tightly using more egg wash, if necessary.

4 Fill a wok or medium-sized pot halfway up with canola oil and bring to 350°F. Add eggrolls and deep-fry until golden brown and crispy. Remove eggrolls and place on paper towel to allow excess oil to drain.

5 Serve finger eggrolls with dipping sauce.

4 인분

170 g	갈은 새우
170 g	갈은 돼지고기
3 큰술	다진 파슬리
3 큰술	다진 샬롯 (양파)
3 큰술	피넛버터
1/2 작은술	소금
적당량	후추
6 개	라이스 페이퍼
1 개분	달걀물
적당량	카놀라 오일

찍어 먹는 소스
스윗 앤 사워 소스 7 큰술, 레몬즙 1½ 큰술,
다진 파슬리 2 큰술, 설탕 1/2 큰술, 후추 적당량

준비 과정

1 찍어 먹는 소스 재료를 한데 섞어둡니다.

2 큰 볼에 새우, 돼지고기, 파슬리, 샬롯, 피넛버터, 소금, 후추를 넣고 잘 섞어둡니다.

3 반으로 자른 직사각형 라이스 페이퍼에 달걀물을 풀어 가장자리 둘레를 바르고 섞어둔 내용물을 손가락 정도의 크기와 모양이 되도록 길게 넣고 한 번 돌린 후 양끝을 안으로 접고 다시 끝까지 돌려 말아줍니다. 끝이 잘 붙지 않으면 달걀물을 좀 더 발라 잘 붙도록 합니다.

4 깊이가 깊은 프라이팬에 기름을 175℃로 달굽니다. 만들어 놓은 핑거 에그롤을 기름에 한 번 튀긴 후 더 바삭하도록 한 번 더 튀깁니다. 꺼내서 기름이 빠지도록 종이타월 위에 둡니다.

5 접시에 담거나 컵에 꽂아 찍어 먹는 소스를 곁들여 상에 냅니다.

Fried Dumplings Twigim Mandu
튀김만두

4 Servings

4 oz.	Green bean sprouts
4 oz.	Zucchini, julienned
2 oz.	Beef, ground
2 oz.	Pork, ground
4 oz.	Firm tofu, squeezed
1 Tbsp	Oyster sauce
1 tsp	Sesame oil
1 Tbsp	Garlic, minced
1/4 Tbsp	Ginger, minced
TT*	Salt, pepper
12	Jumbo gyoza wrappers
1	Egg, whipped (egg wash)
As needed	Canola oil

Dipping Sauce

7 Tbsp	Sweet and sour sauce
1½ Tbsp	Lemon juice
2 Tbsp	Parsley, chopped
1/2 Tbsp	Sugar
TT*	Pepper

*TT : To Taste

Preparation

1 Combine dipping sauce ingredients in a small bowl. Set aside.

2 Bring water to a boil in a large pot. Blanch green bean sprouts for 1 minute and squeeze out excess water. Rough chop the sprouts.

3 Season zucchini with salt and pepper.

4 In a large bowl, combine sprouts and zucchini with ground beef, ground pork, tofu, oyster sauce, sesame oil, garlic, ginger, salt, and pepper.

5 Brush the sides of a gyoza wrapper with egg wash. Place 1~2 tablespoons of filling in the center of the wrapper. Fold the wrapper over and seal the edges well.

6 Fill a wok or medium pot halfway up with canola oil and bring to 375°F. Add dumplings and deep-fry until golden brown and crispy. Remove dumplings and place on paper towel to allow excess oil to drain.

7 Serve dumplings with dipping sauce.

4 인분

110 g	숙주나물
110 g	애호박
60 g	갈은 쇠고기
60 g	갈은 돼지고기
110 g	꽉 짠 부침용 두부
1 큰술	굴소스
1 작은술	참기름
1 큰술	다진 마늘
1/4 큰술	다진 생강
적당량	소금, 후추
12 장	만두피
1 개분	달걀물
적당량	카놀라 오일

찍어 먹는 소스

스윗 앤 사워 소스 7 큰술, 레몬즙 1½ 큰술,
다진 파슬리 2 큰술, 설탕 1/2 큰술, 후추 적당량

준비 과정

1 찍어 먹는 소스 재료를 한데 섞어둡니다.

2 숙주나물은 끓는 물에 살짝 데쳐 꺼내서 물기를 꽉 짜내어 2~3 등분으로 자릅니다.

3 호박은 채 썰어 소금과 후추로 살짝 간합니다.

4 큰 볼에 숙주, 호박, 쇠고기, 돼지고기, 두부, 굴소스, 참기름, 마늘, 생강, 소금, 후추를 넣고 버무려 만두속을 만듭니다.

5 만두피 가장자리에 달걀물을 바른 후 1~2큰술 정도의 만두 속을 채우고 반으로 접어 끝을 붙여 만두를 만듭니다.

6 깊이가 깊은 팬에 카놀라 오일을 넣고 190℃로 기름이 달궈지면 만두를 넣어 겉이 노릇해질 때까지 튀깁니다. 더욱 바삭한 튀김을 위해 한 번 더 튀깁니다. 튀겨낸 만두는 종이타월에 기름이 빠지도록 둡니다.

7 튀김만두와 찍어 먹는 소스를 상에 냅니다.

Pork and Chive Dumplings
돼지고기 부추만두

4 Servings

1/2 lb.	Pork, ground
1½ cup	Korean chives, chopped
1 Tbsp	Scallion, chopped
1 Tbsp	Garlic, minced
1 tsp	Ginger, minced
1 Tbsp	Sesame oil
2 Tbsp	Sesame seeds
1 tsp	Oyster sauce
1/4 tsp	Salt
TT*	Pepper
20 pieces	Wonton wrappers
1	Egg, whipped (egg wash)

Dipping Sauce

1 Tbsp	Soy sauce
1/2 Tbsp	Vinegar
1/2 Tbsp	Lemon juice
1/2 tsp	Sugar
TT*	Pepper or red pepper powder

*TT : To Taste

Preparation

1 Combine dipping sauce ingredients in a small bowl. Set aside.

2 Combine pork, chives, scallion, garlic, ginger, sesame oil, sesame seeds, oyster sauce, salt, and pepper in a large bowl.

3 Brush the edge of a wonton wrapper with egg wash. Place 1~2 tablespoons of the filling in the wrapper. Fold the wrapper over and seal the edges well.

4 Bring a large pot of water to a boil and add dumplings. Cook until dumplings float to the surface (dumplings can also be steamed).

5 Serve dumplings with dipping sauce.

Tip American chives can be substituted for Korean chives.

4인분

225 g	갈은 돼지고기
1½ 컵	한국 부추
1 큰술	다진 파
1 큰술	다진 마늘
1 작은술	다진 생강
1 큰술	참기름
2 큰술	참깨
1 작은술	굴소스
1/4 작은술	소금
적당량	후추
20 장	만두피
1 개분	달걀물

찍어 먹는 소스

간장 1 큰술, 식초 1/2 큰술, 레몬즙 1/2 큰술,
설탕 1/2 작은술, 후추나 고춧가루 적당량

준비 과정

1 찍어 먹는 소스 재료를 한데 섞어둡니다.

2 큰 볼에 돼지고기, 부추, 파, 마늘, 생강, 참기름, 참깨, 굴소스, 소금, 후추를 넣고 잘 섞어 만두 속을 준비합니다.

3 만두피 가장자리에 달걀물을 바른 후 만두속을 1~2큰술 정도 채워 넣고 반으로 접어 끝을 붙여 만두를 만듭니다.

4 큰 냄비에 물을 끓여 만두를 넣고 만두가 떠오르면 건져냅니다 (만두를 쪄도 됩니다).

5 부추만두에 찍어 먹는 소스를 곁들여 상에 냅니다.

Tip 한국 부추를 구하지 못하면 미국 부추를 사용해도 됩니다.

Wonton wrappers 만두피

Spring Roll
스프링 롤

4 Servings

6	Spring roll wrappers
8	Shrimp, medium-sized
1	Carrot, julienned 3-inches long
1	Korean yam, julienned 3-inches long
1	Mango, thickly julienned 3-inches long
1	Cucumber, julienned 3-inches long
1 pack	Radish sprouts, roots cut

Dipping Sauce

1 Tbsp	Lemon juice
1 Tbsp	Fish sauce
1 tsp	Chili sauce
1/2 Tbsp	White wine vinegar
1 Tbsp	sugar
2 Tbsp	Water
1/2 tsp	Garlic, minced
1/4 tsp	Ginger, minced

Preparation

1 Combine dipping sauce ingredients in a small bowl. Set aside.

2 Cook shrimp in a large pot of boiling water until just past raw. Remove, rinse, and peel the shells. Cut in half lengthwise and de-vein.

3 Soak spring roll wrappers in warm water until soft (one at a time as you make each roll).

4 Place shrimp, carrots, Korean yam, cucumber, mango, and radish sprouts down the middle of a wrapper (take care not to overstuff the spring roll). Roll the wrapper around the filling and fold the two outer ends toward the middle. Continue to roll the wrapper and seal.

5 Cut spring rolls diagonally across the middle and serve with dipping sauce.

Tip Spring roll wrappers are extremely delicate, so handle with care.

4 인분

6 장	라이스 페이퍼
8 개	새우
1 개분	7cm로 채 썬 당근
1 개분	7cm로 채 썬 한국 고구마
1 개분	7cm로 채 썬 망고
1 개분	7cm로 채 썬 오이
1 팩	무순

찍어 먹는 소스
레몬즙 1 큰술, 피시소스 1 큰술, 칠리소스 1 작은술,
화이트와인 식초 1/2 큰술, 설탕 1큰술, 물 2 큰술,
다진 마늘 1/2 작은술, 다진 생강 1/4 작은술

준비 과정

1 찍어 먹는 소스 재료를 한데 섞어둡니다.

2 끓는 물에 새우를 삶아서 건져내 잘 헹굽니다. 껍질을 벗기고 세로로 반을 잘라 등 쪽의 내장을 제거합니다.

3 라이스 페이퍼는 롤을 만들기 바로 전에 따뜻한 물에 한 장씩 담갔다가 부드러워지면 꺼내서 씁니다.

4 준비된 라이스 페이퍼 가운데에 새우, 당근, 고구마, 오이, 망고, 무순을 올려놓고 한 번 돌돌 말아준 후 양옆을 안으로 오므리고 다시 끝까지 돌돌 말아줍니다.

5 말아준 스프링 롤은 사선으로 잘라 찍어 먹는 소스와 함께 상에 냅니다.

Tip 라이스 페이퍼는 잘 찢어지므로 조심스럽게 다룹니다.

Spring roll wrappers 라이스 페이퍼

Shrimp and Crab Meat Stuffed Avocado
새우와 게살이 들어간 아보카도

6 Servings

3	Avocados
6	Shrimp, medium-sized, cooked
4 oz.	Crab meat
2 Tbsp	Celery, chopped fine
2 Tbsp	Carrot, chopped fine
2 Tbsp	Water chestnut, chopped fine

Seasoning

5~6 Tbsp	Mayonnaise
TT*	Salt, white pepper

*TT : To Taste

Preparation

1 Blot dry shrimp and crab meat with paper towel. Chop fine and let sit on paper towel for a few minutes to allow excess water to drain.

2 Squeeze water from chopped celery, carrot, and water chestnut and let sit on paper towel for a few minutes.

3 Combine shrimp, crab meat, celery, carrot, and water chestnut with mayonnaise, salt, and white pepper in a large bowl.

4 Cut avocados in half lengthwise and remove the pits.

5 Overstuff the openings left by the pits with the shrimp and crab meat mixture.

6 Shape the stuffing mixture with a spoon and serve.

6 인분

3 개	아보카도
170 g	중간 크기 익은 새우
110 g	게살
2 큰술	잘게 다진 셀러리
2 큰술	잘게 다진 당근
2 큰술	잘게 다진 워터체스넛

양념

마요네즈 5~6 큰술, 소금 · 흰 후추 적당량

준비 과정

1 새우와 게살을 종이타월에 올려두고 물기를 완전히 빼줍니다. 물기를 뺀 새우와 게살을 잘게 다진 후 물기가 빠지도록 다시 종이타월에 올려 둡니다.

2 셀러리, 당근, 워터체스넛은 가능한 한 잘게 다져 물기를 꼭 짜 종이타월에 올려둡니다.

3 다진 새우, 게살, 셀러리, 당근, 워터체스넛을 큰 볼에 넣고, 분량의 마요네즈와 소금, 흰 후추를 넣은 후 재료가 서로 잘 붙을 만큼 골고루 섞어줍니다.

4 아보카도를 씻어 반으로 자른 후 아보카도 씨를 제거합니다. 속의 씨까지 깊숙이 칼을 넣어 자른 후 옆으로 살짝 돌려주면 아보카도 씨를 쉽게 뺄 수 있습니다.

5 씨가 파인 부분에 마요네즈에 버무린 속재료를 넣어 채우고 동그랗게 위로 올라오도록 모양을 내줍니다.

6 작은 수저를 사용해 모양을 다듬어 상에 냅니다.

Tofu Stuffed Baked Clams
대합구이

8 Serving

12	Big clams
2 oz.	Firm tofu, squeezed
2 oz.	Beef, ground
2	Shitake mushrooms, chopped
As needed	Parmesan cheese
4 Tbsp	Parsley, chopped
As needed	Olive oil

Seasoning

1	Egg yolk
1½ tsp	Sugar
1 tsp	Garlic, minced
2 Tbsp	Scallion, chopped
1 tsp	Sesame oil
1 Tbsp	Sesame seeds
TT*	Salt, pepper

*TT : To Taste

Preparation

1 Soak clams in water for 30 minutes. Remove and place in a large pot of boiling water until clams have opened. Remove and pick meat from the shells and set shells aside. Chop clam meat into small pieces.

2 Pick the four largest and cleanest shells. Rinse and split shells into halves.

3 Mix chopped clams with tofu, ground beef, mushrooms, and seasoning ingredients.

4 Brush olive oil inside each shell and slightly overstuff each shell with clam mixture. Sprinkle parmesan cheese over the stuffing.

5 Bake stuffed shells at 400°F for about 15 minutes or until golden brown.

6 Serve stuffed clams garnished with chopped parsley.

Tip ¹ For a little more kick, add hot sauce to clam mixture before stuffing shells.

² Egg wash can be substituted for parmesan cheese.

---

8 인분

12 개	대합
60 g	부침용 두부
60 g	갈은 쇠고기
2 개	다진 표고버섯
적당량	파마산 치즈가루
4 큰술	다진 파슬리
적당량	올리브오일

양념
달걀노른자 1 개, 설탕 1½ 작은술, 다진 마늘 1 작은술, 다진 파 2 큰술, 참기름 1 작은술, 참깨 1 큰술, 소금 · 후추 적당량

준비 과정

1 물에 대합을 30분 정도 담가 해감을 토하게 한 후 끓는 물에 대합을 삶습니다. 대합이 입을 벌리면 건져낸 다음 조갯살만 뽑아서 다집니다. 대합 껍질은 버리지 말고 모아둡니다.

2 가장 크고 깨끗한 대합 껍질 4개를 골라 깨끗이 씻은 후 8개의 조개 껍질이 나오도록 반을 나누어 둡니다.

3 두부도 거즈를 사용해 물기를 꼭 짠 후, 다진 조갯살과 갈은 쇠고기, 버섯, 분량의 양념을 넣고 함께 버무려 줍니다.

4 대합 껍질 속에 올리브오일을 바르고 준비된 조갯살 믹스를 껍질 속에 담아 살짝 올라올 정도로 채워 넣습니다. 조갯살 믹스를 다 덮을 정도로 파마산 치즈가루를 뿌려 둡니다.

5 200℃로 예열된 오븐에 노릇할 때까지 15분 정도 구워냅니다.

6 다진 파슬리로 장식해 상에 냅니다.

Tip ¹ 더 매콤한 맛을 원하면 타바스코 소스를 뿌려 드시면 좋습니다.

² 치즈를 좋아하지 않는 분들은 달걀물을 발라 그냥 구워도 맛있습니다.

Grilled King Oyster Mushroom Skewers

새송이 꼬치

4 Servings

10 oz.	Beef, cut into 1x3-inch slices
1 lb.	Fresh king oyster mushrooms, cut into 1x3-inch pieces
4 stalks	Scallion, cut into 3-inch pieces
12	Wood skewers
As needed	Olive oil

Seasoning

2 Tbsp	Soy sauce
1 Tbsp	Water
1 Tbsp	Brown sugar
1 tsp	Garlic, minced
1 tsp	Sesame oil
TT*	Pepper

*TT : To Taste

Preparation

1 Soak wood skewers in water.

2 Combine beef and seasoning ingredients in a large bowl and let marinate in refrigerator for at least 1 hour.

3 Place on each skewer one piece of mushroom, one slice of meat, one piece of scallion, another slice of meat, and another slice of mushroom.

4 Grill skewers over medium-high heat until beef reaches desired doneness (skewers can also be pan-fried).

5 Serve skewers immediately.

4 인분

280 g	두께 2.5cm, 길이 7cm로 썬 쇠고기
450 g	두께 2.5cm, 길이 7cm로 썬 새송이버섯
4 줄기	7cm 길이로 썬 파
12 개	나무 꼬치
적당량	올리브오일

고기 양념

간장 2 큰술, 물 1 큰술, 흑설탕 1 큰술, 다진 마늘 1 작은술, 참기름1 작은술, 후추 적당량

준비 과정

1 나무 꼬치 12개를 물에 담가 둡니다.

2 쇠고기는 양념에 한 시간 정도 재둡니다.

3 나무 꼬치 하나에 버섯, 고기, 파, 고기, 버섯 순서로 꽂습니다.

4 그릴을 준비해 준비된 고치를 놓고 고기가 익을 때까지 앞뒤로 구워줍니다(기름을 두른 프라이팬에 구워도 됩니다).

5 그릴에서 내린 꼬치를 바로 드셔야 좋습니다.

Oyster Shot
굴회

4 Servings

8	Oysters, removed from shells
4	Quail eggs, yolk only
1 tsp	Pickled ginger, chopped fine
2 tsp	Scallion, chopped fine
TT*	Salt

Sauce

1 tsp	Soy sauce
1 tsp	Vinegar
1 tsp	Lemon juice
2 tsp	Water
1/8 tsp	Sugar

*TT : To Taste

Preparation

1 Combine sauce ingredients in a small bowl. Set aside.

2 Soak oysters in salt water. Remove and strain excess water.

3 Drop two oysters in a shot glass and place egg yolk on top.

4 Add a pinch of pickled ginger, scallion, and 1 teaspoon of sauce to the shot glass.

5 Serve oyster shot immediately.

4 인분

8 개	굴
4 개	메추리알
1 작은술	잘게 다진 절인 생강
2 작은술	잘게 다진 파
적당량	소금

소스

간장 1 작은술, 식초 1 작은술, 레몬즙 1 작은술,
물 2 작은술, 설탕 1/8 작은술

준비 과정

1 소스 재료를 한데 섞어 둡니다.

2 굴을 소금물에 잠시 담갔다 건져둡니다.

3 칵테일 잔에 굴을 두 개씩 담고 그 위에 메추리알 노른자를 올립니다.

4 잘게 다진 생강과 다진 파를 올리고 섞어 둔 소스 1작은술을 넣어 줍니다.

5 바로 드셔야 좋습니다.

Korean Beef Tartare Yuk Hwae

육회

4 Servings

1 lb.	Lean beef
1	Asian pear, julienned
2 stalks	Scallion, chopped
TT*	Pine nuts, crushed
TT*	Salt, pepper, sugar

Seasoning

1 Tbsp	Soy sauce
2 Tbsp	Sugar
1 Tbsp	Scallion, chopped
1 Tbsp	Garlic, minced
1 Tbsp	Sesame oil
1 Tbsp	Sesame seeds
1 tsp	Salt
1/4 tsp	Pepper

*TT : To Taste

Preparation

1 Place beef in freezer for 1 hour. Remove and slice beef into thin strips.

2 Mix beef and seasoning ingredients in a medium-sized bowl.

3 Serve beef arranged over pears. Garnish with chopped scallion and crushed pine nuts.

Tip This dish is traditionally served with a raw quail egg yolk placed over the beef.

4 인분

450 g	쇠고기 우둔살이나 홍두깨살
1 개분	채 썬 아시안 배
2 줄기	다진 파
적당량	잣가루, 소금, 후추, 설탕

고기 양념

간장 1 큰술, 설탕 2 큰술, 다진 파 1 큰술, 다진 마늘 1 큰술,
참기름 1 큰술, 참깨 1 큰술, 소금 1 작은술,
후추 1/4 작은술

준비 과정

1 고기는 냉동실에 넣어 썰기 좋게 살짝 얼린 상태에서 꺼내 가늘게 썬 후 차갑게 보관합니다.

2 먹기 직전 고기와 양념을 볼에 넣고 버무립니다.

3 채 썬 배를 밑에 돌려서 깔고 고기를 올린 다음 파와 잣가루를 올려 상에 냅니다.

Tip 메추리알 노른자를 채 썬 고기 위에 올려 함께 버무려 드셔도 좋습니다.

Korean meals do not typically include Western style salads. Western traditions, however, have influenced the Korean culinary scene, and salads have begun to appear more frequently in Korean menus. Koreans have adapted the Western style salad to suit their Eastern tastes. The following recipes reflect our own efforts to give this Western staple a uniquely Asian twist.

한국 사람들은 서양식 샐러드 대신 보통 반찬과 김치 종류를 놓고 식사를 합니다. 그러나 서양음식과 조리방법들이 응용되면서 요새는 한국음식 메뉴에서도 샐러드 종류를 많이 볼 수 있습니다. 미국에 오래 살면서, 그리고 가족의 건강을 신경쓰느라 식사 때마다 샐러드를 많이 만들어 먹는데, 한국의 맛을 살리면서도 서양음식에 어울리는 레시피들을 소개합니다.

Salads

샐러드

Mung Bean Jelly with Vegetables 탕평채

Smoked Salmon Radish Roll 무쌈 냉채

Tofu with Ham and Orange 햄과 오렌지를 곁들인 두부냉채

Jellyfish Salad with Shrimp 해파리 겨자채

Spring Mix Salad with Sliced Beef 로스편채

Potato Salad 감자 샐러드

Belgian Endives with Shrimp 새우를 곁들인 엔다이브 샐러드

Shellfish Ceviche 해산물 샐러드

Spaghetti Squash Salad 호박국수 샐러드

Broccoli Salad 브로콜리

Red Cabbage Salad 적양배추 샐러드

Mung Bean Jelly with Vegetables
탕평채

4 Servings

1 lb.	Mung bean jelly, julienned
4 oz.	Beef rib eye, julienned
2	Kirby cucumber, julienned
1/2	Carrot, julienned
2 sheets	Dried seaweed
1	Egg, cooked into omelet and sliced thin
TT*	Salt, vinegar, sesame oil
1 Tbsp	Vegetable oil

Seasoning

1/2 Tbsp	Soy sauce
1/2 tsp	Sesame oil
1 tsp	Sugar
1/4 tsp	Garlic, minced
TT*	Salt, pepper

Sauce

1 Tbsp	Soy sauce
1/2 Tbsp	Vinegar
1 Tbsp	Scallion, chopped
1 tsp	Sesame oil
1 tsp	Sugar
1 Tbsp	Sesame seeds
TT*	Salt

*TT : To Taste

Preparation

1 Mix sauce ingredients in a small bowl. Set aside.

2 Boil mung bean jelly for 1~2 minutes. Rinse with cold water and drain. Toss gently in salt and sesame oil.

3 Combine beef and seasoning ingredients and let marinate for at least 1 hour. Heat vegetable oil in a pan over medium-high heat and cook beef until desired doneness.

4 Lightly season cucumber with salt and vinegar for 15 minutes. Squeeze out excess water. Heat vegetable oil in a pan over medium heat and lightly sauté cucumbers.

5 Heat vegetable oil in a pan over medium heat and lightly sauté carrots. Season with salt.

6 Toast seaweed over a gas or electric range and crumble.

7 Combine mung bean jelly, beef, cucumber, carrot, and egg omelet with sauce and serve garnished with crumbled dried seaweed.

Mung bean jelly 청포묵

4 인분

450 g	채 썬 청포묵
110 g	채 썬 쇠고기
2 개분	채 썬 오이
1/2 개분	채 썬 당근
2 장	마른 김
1 개분	달걀지단
적당량	소금, 식초, 참기름
1 큰술	식용유

고기 양념

간장 1/2 큰술, 참기름 1/2 작은술, 설탕 1 작은술,
다진 마늘 1/4 작은술, 소금 · 후추 적당량

양념

간장 1 큰술, 식초 1/2 큰술, 다진 파 1 큰술,
참기름 1 작은술, 설탕 1 작은술, 참깨 1 큰술, 소금 적당량

준비 과정

1 분량의 양념을 볼에 담아 한데 섞어 둡니다.

2 가늘게 채 썬 청포묵은 뜨거운 물에 1~2분 정도 데쳐 건져낸 후 찬물을 끼얹고 물기를 빼 소금과 참기름으로 살짝 버무려 둡니다.

3 채 썬 고기는 고기 양념에 한 시간 정도 재어둔 다음 식용유를 두른 프라이팬에 살짝 볶아 둡니다.

4 채 썬 오이는 소금과 식초로 살짝 버무려 15분 정도 둔 후 물기를 꼭 짜서 살짝 볶아줍니다.

5 채 썬 당근은 소금을 살짝 뿌려 기름에 볶아둡니다.

6 마른 김은 구워서 비닐봉지에 넣고 부숴 둡니다.

7 큰 볼에 청포묵, 고기, 오이채, 당근, 달걀지단을 넣고 먹기 직전에 양념에 버무린 후 마른 김을 위에 뿌려 상에 냅니다.

Smoked Salmon Radish Roll
무쌈 냉채

4 Servings (16 pieces)

1/2 lb.	Korean radish, peeled
1/4	Red onion, sliced thin
1/2	Asian pear, julienned 2 $\frac{1}{2}$ - inches long
1/2	Carrot, julienned 2 $\frac{1}{2}$ -inches long
1 pack	Radish sprouts, roots removed
1/3 lb.	Smoked salmon, cut into 2-inch slices

Radish Vinegar Water

1/2 cup	Water
1/2 cup	Triple sec (optional)
1/2 cup	Vinegar
2 Tbsp	Sugar
1 Tbsp	Salt

Sauce

2 Tbsp	Plain cream cheese
2 Tbsp	Lemon juice
2 Tbsp	Red onion, chopped
3 Tbsp	Olive oil
1 Tbsp	Red wine vinegar
1/4 tsp	Salt

*TT : To Taste

Preparation

1 Blend sauce ingredients in a blender. Set aside.

2 Combine vinegar water ingredients in a medium-sized bowl. Cut radish crosswise into thin slices. Place sliced radish in vinegar water and let sit for at least 20~30 minutes (radish will taste best if soaked overnight).

3 Soak red onions in cold water for 10 minutes.

4 Place red onions, radish sprouts, carrots, smoked salmon, and Asian pear on a slice of radish. Drizzle sauce and roll radish over the ingredients.

5 Serve radish rolls with extra sauce on the side.

Tip [1] Orange juice can be substituted for triple sec.

[2] Korean markets sell sliced radish.

[3] Soak sliced radish in wasabi water or beet water for green or red coloring.

Pickled radish 절인 무

4 인분 (16개)

230 g	무
1/4 개분	가늘게 채 썬 적양파
1/2 개분	6 cm로 채 썬 배
1/2 개분	6 cm로 채 썬 당근
1 팩	무순
150 g	5 cm로 자른 훈제 연어

무 단촛물
물 1/2 컵, 트리플 섹 1/2 컵(선택), 식초 1/2 컵,
설탕 2 큰술, 소금 1 큰술

소스
플레인 크림치즈 2 큰술 , 레몬즙 2 큰술,
다진 적양파 2 큰술, 올리브오일 3 큰술,
레드와인 식초 1 큰술, 소금 1/4 작은술

준비 과정

1 소스 재료를 블렌더에 넣고 갈아둡니다.

2 무는 동그란 모양이 나오게 가로로 얇게 썰어 단촛물에 20~30분 정도 담가둡니다(하루 전날 담가뒀다 쓰면 맛이 배어 더 좋습니다). 무를 단촛물에서 건져 체에 받쳐 물기를 빼둡니다.

3 가늘게 채 썬 적양파는 물에 담가 매운맛을 뺀 후 건져냅니다.

4 무 위에 무순, 당근, 연어, 양파, 배를 올린 다음 소스를 위에 뿌리고 양쪽에서 말아 올려 모양을 냅니다.

5 소스와 함께 곁들여 상에 내놓습니다.

Tip [1] 단촛물에 트리플 섹을 쓰면 오렌지 향이 납니다.

[2] 트리플 섹이 없으면 오렌지주스를 넣어도 됩니다.

[3] 무쌈은 시중에 만들어 놓은 것을 사용하면 더욱 편리합니다.

[4] 무를 초록색, 붉은색으로 내려면 얇게 썬 무를 와사비와 비트물에 각각 넣어 두면 됩니다.

Tofu with Ham and Orange

햄과 오렌지를 곁들인 두부냉채

4 Servings

1 pkg.	Tofu, cut into 1/2-inch cubes
3.5 oz.	Spring mix salad
1	Orange, cut into supremes
4 oz.	Ham, cut into 1/2-inch cubes
1	Red onion, sliced thin lengthwise

Dressing

7 Tbsp	Greek or plain yogurt
2 Tbsp	Orange juice
2 Tbsp	Sugar
2 Tbsp	Olive oil
2 Tbsp	White wine vinegar
2 tsp	Garlic, minced
TT*	Salt, Pepper

*TT : To Taste

Preparation

1 Blend dressing ingredients in a blender until smooth in consistency. Set aside.

2 Soak red onions in cold water for at least 10 minutes.

3 Blanch tofu and set aside.

4 Arrange orange supremes, tofu, ham, and red onion slices over spring mix salad.

5 Drizzle dressing over salad and serve.

4 인분

1 팩	두부
100 g	샐러드 믹스
1 개	살만 발라낸 오렌지
115 g	깍둑썰기 한 햄
1 개분	가로로 가늘게 저며 썬 적양파

드레싱

플레인 요구르트 7 큰술, 오렌지주스 2 큰술, 설탕 2 큰술,
올리브오일 2 큰술, 화이트와인 식초 2 큰술,
마늘 2 작은술, 소금 · 후추 적당량

준비 과정

1 드레싱 재료를 모두 블렌더에 넣고 갈아둡니다.

2 양파는 매운맛이 빠지도록 차가운 물에 10분 정도 담근 후 물기를 빼고 건져둡니다.

3 두부는 살짝 데쳐 찬물에 헹군 후 물기를 뺀 후 깍둑썰기를 해줍니다.

4 샐러드 믹스를 맨 아래 깔고 과육만 발라낸 오렌지와 두부, 햄, 양파를 올립니다.

5 드레싱을 뿌려 상에 냅니다.

Jellyfish Salad with Shrimp

해파리 겨자채

4 Servings

1 lb.	Jelly fish
12	Medium-sized shrimp
1	Cucumber, seedless

Dressing

1 Tbsp	Lemon juice
3 Tbsp	Pine nuts
1 Tbsp	Korean mustard
2 tbsp	Garlic, minced
3 Tbsp	Sugar
1/2 tbsp	Salt
2 Tbsp	Water
TT*	Pepper

*TT : To Taste

Preparation

1 Blend dressing ingredients in a blender until smooth in consistency. Set aside.

2 Wash jellyfish in salt water and blanch. Remove and drain.

3 Cook shrimp in boiling water until just past raw. Peel and cut into halves lengthwise.

4 Cut cucumber lengthwise into thin slices (a peeler can be used).

5 Arrange jellyfish and shrimp over cucumber slices. Drizzle dressing over salad and serve garnished with parsley.

4 인분

450 g	해파리
12 개	중새우 (껍질 벗긴 것)
1 개	씨 없는 오이

드레싱

레몬즙 1 큰술, 잣 3 큰술, 겨자 1 큰술, 마늘 2 작은술,
설탕 3 큰술, 소금 1/2 작은술, 물 2 큰술, 후추 적당량

준비 과정

1 드레싱 재료는 블렌더에 넣고 잘 갈아둡니다.

2 해파리는 소금물에 씻은 후 끓는 물에 잠시 데쳐 차가운 물에 담갔다 꺼내 물기를 빼둡니다.

3 새우도 잘 씻어 뜨거운 물에 데친 다음 꺼내 껍질을 벗겨서 길이로 반을 잘라 놓습니다.

4 오이는 둥글납작하게 썰거나, 필러를 사용해 길게 잘라 놓습니다.

5 오이를 접시에 깔고 그 위에 해파리, 새우를 올려 담은 후 파슬리로 장식해 겨자소스와 함께 상에 냅니다.

Jelly fish 해파리

Spring Mix Salad with Sliced Beef
로스편채

4 Servings

2 lb.	Beef tenderloin
2 Tbsp	Montreal seasoning
TT*	Salt
1 pack	Spring mix salad
1 pack	Radish sprouts

Dressing

4 Tbsp	Plain yogurt
2 Tbsp	Lemon juice
1 tsp	Wasabi
1 tsp	Honey
1 tsp	Sugar
1 tsp	Garlic, minced
TT*	Salt, pepper

* TT : To Taste

Preparation

1 Blend dressing ingredients in a blender. Set aside.

2 Sprinkle Montreal seasoning and salt on beef tenderloin and let sit for about 30 minutes. Bake beef tenderloin in a 400°F oven for 1 hour.

3 Remove beef and let rest for 30 minutes. Cut meat into thin slices.

4 Arrange sliced beef around a plate and place spring salad mix and radish sprouts in the middle. Drizzle dressing over salad and serve with extra dressing on the side.

4인분

900 g	쇠고기 허리살
2 큰술	몬트리얼 시즈닝
적당량	소금
1 팩	샐러드 믹스
1 팩	무순

드레싱

플레인 요구르트 4 큰술, 레몬즙 2 큰술, 와사비 1 작은술, 꿀 1 작은술, 설탕 1 작은술, 다진 마늘 1 작은술, 소금·후추 적당량

준비 과정

1 드레싱 재료를 블렌더에 넣고 갈아둡니다.

2 쇠고기에 몬트리얼 시즈닝과 소금을 뿌려 30분 정도 재운 후 미리 달궈진 200℃의 오븐에 1시간 정도 구워 냅니다.

3 구워진 고기를 꺼내 30분 정도 식힌 후 얇게 썰어줍니다.

4 썬 고기를 접시 가장자리에 돌려 놓고, 샐러드 믹스나 무순을 가운데 올린 후 준비된 드레싱을 뿌립니다. 드레싱은 따로 옆에 더 담아 고기와 샐러드를 먹을 때 조금씩 찍어 먹을 수 있도록 같이 상에 냅니다.

Tip 몬트리얼 시즈닝이 없으면 소금과 후추를 고기 겉 부분에 골고루 뿌려 30분 정도 둔 후 구워줍니다.

Potato Salad
감자 샐러드

4 Servings

2	Potatoes, cut into small cubes
1	Carrots, cut into small cubes
1/2 cup	Frozen green peas
1	Granny Smith apple, cut into small cubes
1	Cucumber, cut into small cubes
3	Hard-boiled eggs, chopped

Dressing

3 Tbsp	Mayonnaise
2 Tbsp	Lemon juice
1 Tbsp	Sugar
1/2 Tbsp	Salt
TT*	Pepper

*TT : To Taste

Preparation

1 Boil potatoes and carrots with a pinch of salt until soft. Remove, drain, and set aside.

2 Season diced cucumbers and apples with salt.

3 Blanch frozen green peas.

4 Toss potatoes, carrots, cucumbers, apples, green peas, and boiled eggs with dressing. Season with salt and pepper as needed.

5 Serve warm or chilled.

Tip This potato salad also works great in sandwiches.

4 인분

2 개분	깍둑 썬 감자
1 개분	깍둑 썬 당근
1/2 컵	냉동 완두콩
1 개분	깍둑 썬 사과
1 개분	깍둑 썬 오이
3 개분	잘게 썬 삶은 달걀

드레싱
마요네즈 3 큰술, 레몬즙 2 큰술, 설탕 1 큰술,
소금 1/2큰술, 후추 적당량

준비 과정

1 감자와 당근은 소금을 약간 넣어 삶아줍니다. 감자와 당근이 익으면 건져 둡니다.

2 오이와 사과에 소금을 약간 뿌려둡니다.

3 냉동 완두콩도 살짝 데쳐둡니다.

4 감자, 당근, 오이, 사과, 완두콩, 삶은 달걀을 한데 담고 분량의 드레싱에 버무린 다음 소금과 후추로 간을 맞춥니다.

5 따뜻하게 드셔도 좋고 차갑게 드셔도 좋습니다.

Tip 샌드위치로 만들어 먹어도 좋습니다.

Belgian Endives with Shrimp

새우를 곁들인 엔다이브 샐러드

4 Servings (8 pieces)

2	Belgian endives
1	Red bell pepper
1	Orange bell pepper
1	Mango
1/4 lb.	Small shrimp, cooked

Dressing

1 Tbsp	Soy sauce
1 Tbsp	White wine vinegar
1 Tbsp	Lemon Juice
1/4 tsp	Wasabi
1 tsp	Honey
TT*	Salt, pepper

*TT : To Taste

Preparation

1 Combine dressing ingredients in a bowl. Set aside.

2 Rinse endives and carefully remove the leaves. Blot dry with paper towel.

3 Dice red and orange bell peppers and mango.

4 Place one shrimp and equal amounts of bell peppers and mango on each endive.

5 Serve endives with dressing on the side.

Tip Sashimi tuna can be substituted for shrimp.

4 인분 (8개)

2개	엔다이브
1개	홍피망
1개	주황피망
1개	망고
115g	작은 새우 익은 것

드레싱

간장 1 큰술, 화이트와인 식초 1 큰술, 레몬즙 1 큰술,
와사비 1/4 작은술, 꿀 1 작은술, 소금 · 후추 적당량

준비 과정

1 드레싱 재료를 한데 섞어 둡니다.

2 엔다이브를 잘 씻어 잎을 한 장씩 떼어낸 후 종이타월로 물기를 잘 닦아 놓습니다.

3 홍피망, 주황 피망, 망고를 작은 크기로 깍둑썰기 합니다.

4 엔다이브 잎 한 장에 홍피망, 주황피망, 망고, 새우를 올립니다.

5 엔다이브 샐러드를 예쁘게 배열하고 드레싱을 올려 상에 냅니다.

Tip 새우 대신 참치회를 사용해도 좋습니다.

Shellfish Ceviche

해산물 샐러드

4 Servings

4	Scallops
1 Tbsp	Lemon juice
4 oz.	Octopus, cooked
8	Medium-sized shrimp, cooked
1 Tbsp	Parsley, chopped
1 Tbsp	Chives, chopped
1 Tbsp	Scallion, chopped
TT*	Salt, pepper
As needed	Olive oil

Sauce

2 Tbsp	Red pepper paste
1 Tbsp	Vinegar
1/2 Tbsp	Lemon juice
1 Tbsp	Water
1 tsp	Sugar
1 tsp	Sesame seeds
TT*	Salt, pepper

*TT : To Taste

Preparation

1 Combine sauce ingredients in a bowl. Set aside.

2 Season scallops with salt, pepper, and lemon juice. Let sit for 10 minutes then grill to desired doneness.

3 Grill or pan-fry scallops over medium-high heat until desired doneness.

4 Cut cooked octopus into bite-sized pieces and toss with grilled scallops, shrimp, parsley, chives, and scallion.

5 Drizzle ceviche with sauce and serve.

Tip Light vegetables can be added to the cheviche.

4 인분

4개	관자
적당량	소금, 후추
1 큰술	레몬즙
115 g	익은 문어
8개	중간 크기 익은 새우
1 큰술	다진 파슬리
1 큰술	다진 차이브
1 큰술	다진 파
적당량	올리브오일

소스

고추장 2 큰술, 식초 1 큰술, 레몬즙 1/2 큰술, 물 1 큰술,
설탕 1 작은술, 참깨 1 작은술, 소금·후추 적당량

준비 과정

1 소스를 한데 섞어둡니다.

2 관자는 소금, 후추, 레몬즙을 뿌려 10분 정도 두었다가 그릴에 구워냅니다.

3 그릴이나 올리브오일을 두른 프라이팬에 관자를 구워냅니다.

3 문어는 한 입 크기로 썰어 구운 관자, 새우, 파슬리, 차이브, 파와 함께 섞어 접시에 담습니다.

4 먹기 전에 드레싱을 뿌려 상에 냅니다.

Tip 좋아하는 채소를 해물 샐러드에 넣어 드셔도 좋습니다.

Spaghetti Squash Salad
호박국수 샐러드

4 Servings

1	Spaghetti squash
1	Leek

Dressing

3 Tbsp	Red pepper paste
2 Tbsp	White wine vinegar
2 Tbsp	Sprite or other lime soda
1 Tbsp	Brown sugar
1 Tbsp	Corn syrup
1 Tbsp	Leek, chopped
1 tsp	Garlic, minced

* TT : To Taste

Preparation

1 Combine dressing ingredients in a small bowl. Set aside.

2 Cut leek in half and soak in water for 15~20 minutes. Remove, julienne, and set aside.

3 Cut squash in half lengthwise and remove the seeds.

4 Bake squash in a 375°F oven for 45 minutes. Turn off heat and leave squash in oven for 5 more minutes.

5 Once cool, scoop out the squash with a large spoon. Place scooped out squash briefly in an ice water bath. Remove squash and squeeze out excess water.

6 Drizzle squash with dressing and serve garnished with julienned leek.

---

4 인분

1 개	국수호박
1 줄기	5cm 길이로 채 썬 릭 (대파)

드레싱

고추장 3 큰술, 화이트와인 식초 2 큰술, 사이다 2 큰술,
흑설탕 1 큰술, 물엿 1 큰술, 다진 대파 1 큰술,
다진 마늘 1 작은술

준비 과정

1 드레싱 재료를 섞어둡니다.

2 파를 길이로 반 자른 후 물에 15~20분 정도 담가 두었다가 물기를 빼내고 5cm 길이로 채 썹니다.

3 국수호박을 씻어 반으로 잘라 씨를 깨끗이 빼냅니다.

4 호박을 190℃의 오븐에 45분 동안 구워낸 후 오븐을 끄고 5분 정도 안에 둡니다.

5 오븐에서 꺼내 식힌 후 큰 수저로 익은 호박을 모두 파냅니다. 파낸 호박을 얼음물에 잠시 담갔다 건져내 물기를 꼭 짜줍니다.

6 준비한 소스와 스파게티 모양으로 나온 국수호박을 함께 버무려 남은 파로 장식해 상에 냅니다.

Tip ¹ 국수호박을 삶아서 속을 파내 사용해도 됩니다.

² 국수호박은 삶아서 수저로 파내면 국수처럼 결이 생깁니다. 이것을 얼음물에 담갔다 건지면 호박국수가 됩니다.

³ 릭이 없으면 대파를 가늘게 채 썰어 물에 담가 매운맛을 뺀 후 사용하면 됩니다.

Broccoli Salad
브로콜리 샐러드

4 Servings

1	Broccoli
1 stalk	Scallion, cut diagoally
1	Carrot, julienned (optional)

Dressing

1 Tbsp	Fish sauce
1 Tbsp	Dried red pepper powder
1 tsp	Garlic, minced
1/2 tsp	Ginger, minced
1 Tbsp	Scallion, chopped
1 tsp	Sugar
1 tsp	Sesame seeds

Preparation

1 Combine dressing ingredients in a small bowl. Set aside.

2 Bring water and 2 tablespoons of salt to a boil. Blanch broccoli for about 1~2 minutes.

3 Toss broccoli, scallion, and carrots with dressing and serve.

4 인분

1 개	브로콜리
1 줄기	어슷 썬 파
1 개분	채 썬 당근 (선택)

드레싱

피시소스 1 큰술, 고춧가루 1 큰술, 다진 마늘 1 작은술, 다진 생강 1/2 작은술, 다진 파 1 큰술, 설탕 1 작은술, 참깨 1 작은술

준비 과정

1 드레싱에 들어갈 재료를 한데 섞어둡니다.

2 물이 끓으면 소금 2큰술을 넣고 브로콜리를 넣어서 1~2분간 데쳐낸 다음 얼음물에 담갔다 건져 냅니다.

3 브로콜리, 파, 당근에 준비된 드레싱을 뿌려 잘 섞어 상에 냅니다.

Red Cabbage Salad

적양배추 샐러드

4 Servings

1/2	Red cabbage, julienned
1 Tbsp	Parsley, chopped

Dressing

3 Tbsp	Olive oil
1 Tbsp	Sherry vinegar
1 Tbsp	Lemon juice
1 Tbsp	Sugar
1 tsp	Garlic, minced
1/2 tsp	Salt
TT*	Salt, Pepper

*TT : To Taste

Preparation

1 Combine dressing ingredients in a large bowl.

2 Toss cabbage with dressing and serve garnished with parsley.

Tip Any wine vinegar can be substituted for sherry vinegar.

4 인분

1/2 개	채 썬 적양배추
1 큰술	다진 파슬리

드레싱

올리브오일 3 큰술, 셰리 비니거 1 큰술, 레몬즙 1 큰술,
설탕 1 큰술, 다진 마늘 1 작은술, 소금 1/2 작은술,
소금 · 후추 적당량

준비 과정

1 드레싱 재료를 한데 섞어둡니다.

2 드레싱을 섞은 볼에 양배추를 넣고 잘 섞은 후 파슬리로 장식해 상에 냅니다.

Tip 셰리 비니거 대신 다른 종류의 식초를 써도 됩니다.

One of my greatest pleasures is to cook hearty meals for my two sons when they come to visit Mom and Dad. Both epic carnivores, my sons almost always request that I fix them their favorite dish, galbi (grilled beef short ribs in a soy-based marinade).

지금은 어른이 다 된 우리 두 아들들이 좋아하는 요리는 역시 고기요리라 아이들이 우리 집을 방문한다 하면 어떤 고기를 해줄까 고민하지요. 그 중 그래도 갈비요리가 최고랍니다.

Meats & Seafood

고기와 해산물

Beef

Bulgogi 불고기

Grilled LA Galbi LA 갈비

Beef with Coriander Seeds 너비아니 구이

Braised Beef Short Ribs Galbi Jjim 갈비찜

Lamb Rib Chops 양갈비 구이

Soy Ginger Veal 송아지고기 구이

Pork

Pork Belly Lettuce Wraps Dwehji Bossam 돼지 보쌈

Miso Pork Mac Jeok 맥적

Grilled Spicy Pork Belly 삼겹살 고추장 구이

Baby Back Ribs 돼지갈비 찜

Ginger Soy Fried Baby Back Ribs 돼지갈비 튀김

Sweet and Sour Pork Tahngsooyook 탕수육

Fried Pork Cutlet Donkasu 돈가스

Tofu with Kimchi and Pork Belly 두부 김치 두루치기

Poultry

Soy Ginger Chicken Drummettes Dahk Ganjung 닭강정

Oregano Chicken 오레가노 향이 나는 닭다리 찜

Spicy Chicken and Potato 닭도리탕

Spicy Chicken Stir Fry with Vegetables Dahk Galbi 닭갈비

Mango Teriyaki Chicken 망고 소스를 곁들인 데리야키 치킨

Seafood

Spicy Scallops 매운 소스를 곁들인 관자구이

Spicy Grilled Shrimp 머리 달린 매운 새우구이

Shrimp with Broccoli 브로콜리를 곁들인 새우볶음

Fried Shrimp and Squid 새우와 오징어 튀김

Stir Fry Spicy Squid Ojinguh Bokum 오징어 볶음

Grilled Mackerel 고등어구이

Sea Bass with Black Bean Sauce 블랙빈 소스를 곁들인 농어

Miso Black Cod 미소 소스 은대구 구이

Spicy Belt Fish 매운 갈치조림

Bulgogi
불고기

4 Servings

2 lb.	Beef rib eye, sliced thin
1	Medium onion, sliced lengthwise
2 stalks	Scallion, chopped
4 rings	Pineapple
As needed	Grapeseed oil, cilantro

Seasoning

4 Tbsp	Soy sauce
4 Tbsp	Sugar
2 Tbsp	Red wine
1 Tbsp	Garlic, minced
2 Tbsp	Scallion, chopped
3 Tbsp	Onion, pureed
1 tsp	Sesame oil
1 tsp	Sesame seeds
TT*	Pepper

*TT : To Taste

Preparation

1 Combine seasoning ingredients in a large bowl. Add beef and let marinate for at least 1 hour.

2 Heat grapeseed oil in a large pan over medium-high heat. Add onions and cook for about two minutes. Add beef and continue cooking, stirring occasionally.

3 When beef is nearly cooked, reduce heat to lowest setting and add chopped scallion. Cook for an additional 2-3 minutes, stirring frequently.

4 Arrange beef over pineapple rings and serve garnished with scallion and cilantro.

Tip [1] Most Korean markets carry sliced rib eye (marinated and unmarinated).

[2] Pureed pear can be added to the beef seasoning for a slightly sweeter and nuttier flavor.

4 인분

900 g	쇠고기 (불고기감)
1 개분	양파(중간 크기 썬 것)
2 줄기	다진 파
4 쪽	파인애플 슬라이스
적당량	포도씨 오일
적당량	실란트로

고기 양념

간장 4 큰술, 설탕 4 큰술, 레드와인 2 큰술, 다진 마늘 1 큰술, 다진 파 2 큰술, 양파즙 3 큰술, 참기름 1 작은술, 참깨 1 작은술, 후추 적당량

준비 과정

1 고기 양념을 잘 섞은 후 쇠고기를 양념에 무쳐서 한 시간 정도 재둡니다.

2 센 불에 달군 프라이팬에 포도씨 오일을 조금 두르고 채 썬 양파를 2분 정도 볶다가 쇠고기를 넣어서 같이 볶아줍니다.

3 고기가 다 익으면 불을 줄인 후 다진 파를 넣고 잠깐 볶습니다.

4 접시에 파인애플과 불고기를 담고 다진 파와 실란트로를 보기 좋게 올려 상에 냅니다.

Tip [1] 쇠고기는 불고기감으로 준비해 둡니다. 불고기감 쇠고기는 한국 마켓에 가면 쉽게 구할 수 있습니다.

[2] 양념에 배즙을 넣으시면 맛이 훨씬 좋습니다.

Grilled LA Galbi
LA 갈비

4 Servings

3 lb.	LA beef short ribs
2 bulbs	Garlic
As needed	Olive oil

Seasoning

6 Tbsp	Soy sauce
4 Tbsp	Sugar
1 Tbsp	Corn syrup
3 Tbsp	Red wine
2 Tbsp	Garlic, minced
1 Tbsp	Ginger, minced
2 Tbsp	Sesame seeds
1 Tbsp	Sesame oil
1 tsp	Pepper
4 Tbsp	Onion, pureed
4 Tbsp	Pear, pureed (optional)
TT*	Salt

*TT : To Taste

Preparation

1 Combine seasoning ingredients in a large bowl.

2 Clean beef short ribs with paper towel. Add short ribs to the seasoning and let marinate in a refrigerator for 3~5 hours.

3 Cut bulbs of garlic in half and brush with olive oil. Roast garlic in a 400°F oven for 20 minutes and set aside.

4 Broil short ribs in a 350°F oven for 20 minutes. Short ribs may also be grilled or cooked in a pan over medium-high heat.

5 Serve short ribs with roasted garlic on the side.

Tip Two tablespoons of pineapple juice can be substituted for pureed pear.

4 인분

1.35 kg	LA 갈비
2 통	통마늘
적당량	올리브오일

갈비 양념

간장 6 큰술, 설탕 4 큰술, 시럽 1 큰술, 레드와인 3 큰술,
다진 마늘 2 큰술, 다진 생강 1 큰술, 참깨 2 큰술,
참기름 1 큰술, 후추 1 작은술, 양파즙 4 큰술,
배즙 4 큰술(선택), 소금 적당량

준비 과정

1 갈비 양념을 볼에 잘 섞어 둡니다.

2 갈비는 페이퍼키친타월로 닦아내고 준비된 갈비 양념에 3~5시간 정도 재둡니다.

3 통마늘을 가로로 반 갈라서 올리브오일을 발라 미리 예열된 200℃ 오븐에 20분간 로스트로 구워 꺼내 놓습니다.

4 갈비를 미리 예열된 190℃ 오븐에 20분 정도 브로일로 구워냅니다. 뜨겁게 달군 프라이팬에 이나 그릴에 직접 구워도 좋습니다.

5 구운 갈비를 오븐에 구워낸 마늘과 함께 상에 냅니다.

Tip 배즙 대신 파인애플 주스 2큰술을 사용해도 됩니다.

Beef with Coriander Seeds
너비아니 구이

4 Servings

1 lb.	Beef filet mignon or rib eye
1 Tbsp	Coriander seeds, crushed
3 Tbsp	Pine nuts, crushed
1 stalk	Scallion, chopped

Seasoning

3 Tbsp	Soy sauce
3 Tbsp	Brown sugar
2 Tbsp	Scallion, chopped
1 Tbsp	Garlic, minced
1 tsp	Ginger, minced
2 Tbsp	Pineapple juice
1 Tbsp	Red wine
1 Tbsp	Sesame oil
1 Tbsp	Sesame seeds
2 Tbsp	Water
TT*	Salt, pepper

*TT : To Taste

Preparation

1 Pound meat with a tenderizing hammer until 1/2-inch thick. Cut meat into 2×3-inch pieces. Coat meat with crushed coriander seeds and let sit for about 15 minutes.

2 Combine seasoning ingredients in a large bowl. Add meat and let marinate in a refrigerator for at least 1 hour.

3 Grill or pan fry marinated meat over high heat until desired doneness. Serve garnished with crushed pine nuts and chopped scallion.

4 인분

450g	쇠고기 안심
1 큰술	잘게 부순 코리앤더 씨
3 큰술	잣가루
1 줄기	다진 파

고기 양념

간장 3 큰술, 흑설탕 3 큰술, 다진 파 2 큰술,
다진 마늘 1 큰술, 다진 생강 1 작은술, 파인애플 주스 2 큰술,
레드와인 1 큰술, 참기름 1 큰술, 참깨 1 큰술, 물 2 큰술,
소금 · 후추 적당량

준비 과정

1 쇠고기는 1cm 두께 정도가 되게 두드려 편 후 가로 5cm 세로 7cm 로 자릅니다. 코리앤더 씨를 앞뒤로 발라 15분간 재둡니다.

2 고기를 분량의 고기 양념에 무쳐서 랩을 씌워 냉장고에 1시간 정도 재둡니다.

3 그릴 위에 앞뒤로 구운 후 잣가루와 송송 썬 파를 올려 모양을 내서 상에 냅니다.

Braised Beef Short Ribs Galbi Jjim
갈비찜

4 Servings

2 lb.	Beef short ribs
1	Onion
4	Dried shitake mushrooms
2	Carrots, cut into 2-inch pieces
10	Chestnuts, drained (optional)
1	Egg, cooked into omelet and sliced thin

Seasoning

1 Tbsp	Rosemary, chopped fine (optional)
5 Tbsp	Soy sauce
5 Tbsp	Onion, pureed
4 Tbsp	Brown sugar
2 Tbsp	Corn syrup
2 Tbsp	Red wine
3 Tbsp	Scallion, chopped
1 Tbsp	Garlic, minced
1 Tbsp	Sesame seeds
1 Tbsp	Sesame oil
TT*	Pepper

*TT : To Taste

Preparation

1 Combine seasoning ingredients in a large bowl. Set aside.

2 Soak mushrooms in water for about 1 hour. Remove mushrooms and cut stem ends. Drain and set aside.

3 Soak short ribs in water for at least 30 minutes and rinse. Place short ribs and onion in a large pot and add enough water to cover. Bring to a boil over high heat for 20 minutes.

4 Remove short ribs and score in 1/2-inch intervals. Strain remaining stock and set aside.

5 Combine short ribs with seasoning. Place short ribs and three cups of stock in a large pot and bring to a boil. Reduce heat to low-medium and cook until stock reduces by half. Add mushrooms, carrots, and chestnuts and continue to simmer over low heat. Stir occasionally. Remove when short ribs are fork tender.

6 Serve short ribs garnished with sliced omelet.

Tip Add dried dates and gingko nuts with mushrooms, carrots, and chestnuts, if in season.

4 인분

900 g	소갈비
1 개	양파
4 개	마른 표고버섯
2 개분	5 cm 길이로 썬 당근
10 개	밤 (선택), 캔이나 팩
1 개분	달걀지단

갈비 양념장

잘게 다진 로즈마리 (선택) 1 큰술, 간장 5 큰술,
갈은 양파 5 큰술, 흑설탕 4 큰술, 물엿이나 시럽 2 큰술,
레드와인 2 큰술, 다진 파 3 큰술, 다진 마늘 1 큰술,
참깨 1 큰술, 참기름 1 큰술, 후추 적당량

준비 과정

1 갈비 양념 재료를 한데 섞어둡니다.

2 마른 표고버섯은 물에 한 시간 정도 담가 불려서 기둥을 떼고 준비해 둡니다.

3 갈비는 30분 정도 물에 담가 핏물을 뺀 후, 큰 냄비에 갈비와 양파를 넣고 갈비가 잠길 만큼 물을 부어 센 불에 20분 정도 끓입니다.

4 갈비를 꺼내 1cm 간격으로 칼집을 넣어두고, 국물은 고운체에 밭쳐 둡니다.

5 냄비에 칼집 넣은 갈비와 준비된 갈비 양념을 섞은 후 갈비 삶은 물 3컵을 붓고 중간 불에 끓입니다. 국물이 반 정도로 줄면 불을 줄이고 표고버섯, 당근, 밤을 넣고 다시 국물이 반으로 줄고 갈비가 부드럽게 다 익었으면 불을 끕니다. 익히는 동안 가끔 저어줍니다.

6 갈비와 표고버섯, 당근, 밤을 담고 달걀지단으로 장식하여 상에 냅니다.

Tip 표고버섯, 당근, 밤을 넣고 끓일 때 대추와 은행을 넣으면 맛이 더 좋습니다.

Lamb Rib Chops
양갈비 구이

4 Serving

8	Lamb rib chops
8 stalks	Asparagus
1/2 lb.	Spring mix salad
As needed	Olive oil

Seasoning

2 $\frac{1}{2}$ Tbsp	Soy sauce
1 $\frac{1}{2}$ Tbsp	Sugar
1 Tbsp	Garlic, minced
1 tsp	Ginger, minced
2 Tbsp	Red wine
1 tsp	Coriander seeds, crushed
1 tsp	Dried thyme
1 tsp	Dried oregano

Preparation

1 Combine seasoning ingredients in a large bowl.

2 Add rib chops and let marinate in refrigerator for 3 hours.

3 Heat oil in a large pan over medium-high heat and add rib chops and asparagus. Cook each side of each rib chop for 4~5 minutes.

4 Serve rib chops and asparagus over spring mix salad.

4 인분

8 대	양갈비
8 줄기	아스파라거스
225 g	샐러드 믹스
적당량	올리브오일

양념

간장 2 $\frac{1}{2}$ 큰술, 설탕 1 $\frac{1}{2}$ 큰술, 다진 마늘 1 큰술,
다진 생강 1 작은술, 레드와인 2 큰술,
잘게 부순 코리앤더 씨 1 작은술, 말린 타임 1 작은술,
말린 오레가노 1 작은술

준비 과정

1 분량의 양념을 볼에 넣어 한데 섞어둡니다.

2 양갈비를 섞어 둔 양념에 재서 3시간 동안 냉장고에 넣어둡니다.

3 프라이팬에 오일을 두르고 양갈비를 앞뒤로 각각 4~5분 정도 구워줍니다. 그릴을 해도 좋습니다. 같은 프라이팬에 아스파라거스도 구워 줍니다.

4 접시에 양갈비와 아스파라거스, 샐러드 믹스를 곁들여 상에 냅니다.

Fresh thyme 타임

Soy Ginger Veal
송아지고기 구이

4 Servings

1 lb.(4 pieces)	Veal, sliced or pounded thin
As needed	Flour, olive oil
1 oz.	Butter, cut in pieces
4 Tbsp	Shallot, chopped fine
4 oz.	Marsala wine
5 oz.	Beef stock
2 Tbsp	Parsley, chopped fine
As needed	Spring salad mix

Seasoning

2 Tbsp	Soy sauce
1 Tbsp	Water
1 tsp	Garlic, minced
1/4 tsp	Ginger, minced
1 tsp	Sugar
TT*	Salt, Pepper

*TT : To Taste

Preparation

1 Combine seasoning ingredients in a large bowl.

2 Add veal and let marinate for 30 minutes.

3 Dredge veal in flour and shake off excess. Heat olive oil and half the butter in a large pan over high heat and cook both sides of veal until golden brown. Set aside.

4 Add olive oil to the same pan and sauté chopped shallots for 2~3 minutes. Add Marsala wine, beef stock, and remaining butter. Simmer until the sauce thickens. Add veal back into the pan and simmer for another minute. Add salt and pepper to taste.

5 Arrange spring salad mix over veal and serve garnished with chopped parsley.

Tip ¹ Any wine can be substituted for marsala wine.

² Onion can be substituted for shallot.

4인분

450 g (4 조각)	송아지 고기
적당량	밀가루, 올리브오일
30 g	버터
4 큰술	다진 샬롯(양파)
115 g	마살라 와인
150 g	쇠고기 육수
2 큰술	다진 파슬리
적당량	샐러드 믹스

고기 양념

간장 2 큰술, 물 1 큰술, 다진 마늘 1 작은술,
다진 생강 1/4 작은술, 설탕 1 작은술, 소금 · 후추 적당량

준비 과정

1 양념 재료를 한데 섞어둡니다.

2 송아지 고기는 30분 정도 미리 양념에 재둡니다.

3 송아지 고기에 밀가루를 묻혀 털어냅니다. 센 불로 달궈진 프라이팬에 올리브오일과 절반의 버터를 넣고 고기를 앞뒤로 구워낸 다음 따로 접시에 담아둡니다.

4 고기를 구운 팬에 올리브오일을 조금 더 넣고 다진 샬롯을 넣어 2~3분 볶은 다음 마살라 와인과 쇠고기 육수, 나머지 버터를 넣고 반으로 줄 때까지 조려 소스를 만듭니다. 여기에 다시 구워둔 송아지 고기를 넣고 약한 불에서 소스와 함께 조리듯이 고기를 굽다가 소금과 후추로 간을 봅니다.

5 송아지 구이를 접시에 담고 그 위에 샐러드 믹스를 올린 후 다진 파슬리로 장식해서 상에 냅니다.

Tip ¹마살라 와인이 없으면 다른 종류의 와인을 사용합니다.

²샬롯을 구하지 못하면 양파로 대체합니다.

4 Servings

2 lb.	Pork belly
7 cloves	Garlic
1 oz.	Ginger
12 cups	Water
2 tsp	Coffee
5	Boston lettuce leaves
5	Bok choy leaves
5	Radicchio leaves
1/2 pack	Radish sprouts
5	Sesame leaves, optional

Salted Shrimp Sauce

1 Tbsp	Salted shrimp sauce
1 Tbsp	Scallion, chopped
1 Tbsp	Celery, chopped
2 tsp	Sesame seeds
1 tsp	Sesame oil

Soybean Paste Sauce

2 Tbsp	Soy paste sauce
2 tsp	Mayonnaise
2 Tbsp	Scallion, chopped
1/2 tsp	Garlic, minced
1/2 tsp	Sugar
1 tsp	Sesame seeds
1 tsp	Sesame oil
1 Tbsp	Pine nuts or almonds, crushed

Preparation

1 Combine salted shrimp sauce and soybean paste sauce ingredients in separate bowls. Set aside.

2 Bring 12 cups of water to a boil in a large pot. Add pork belly, garlic, ginger, and coffee and cook 60 to 75 minutes (blood should not run out of pork if poked).

3 Remove pork and let cool. Slice pork belly into bite-sized pieces.

4 Arrange Boston lettuce, bok choy, radicchio, sesame leaves, radish sprouts, and sliced pork belly on a large plate and serve with sauces. To eat, wrap pork belly in lettuce and add vegetables and sauces as desired.

4 인분

900 g	돼지 삼겹살
7 쪽	마늘
30 g	생강
12 컵	물
2 작은술	커피
5 장	보스턴 레터스
5 장	청경채
5 장	적상추
1/2 팩	무순
5 장	깻잎(선택)

새우젓 소스
새우젓 1 큰술, 다진 파 1 큰술, 셀러리 1 큰술,
참깨 2 작은술, 참기름 1 작은술

된장 소스
된장 2 큰술, 마요네즈 2 작은술, 다진 파 2 큰술,
다진 마늘 1/2 작은술, 설탕 1/2 작은술, 참깨 1 작은술,
참기름 1 작은술, 잣가루나 다진 아몬드 1 큰술

준비 과정

1 새우젓 소스와 된장 소스 재료들을 각각 다른 볼에 섞어둡니다.

2 물 12컵에 돼지고기 삼겹살과 마늘, 생강, 커피를 넣고 1시간에서 1시간 15분 정도 삶아냅니다. 칼로 찔러서 피가 안 날 정도면 됩니다.

3 삶은 고기는 조심스럽게 꺼내 잠시 식힌 후 먹기 좋은 크기로 잘라둡니다.

4 큰 접시에 보스턴 레터스, 청경채, 적상추, 무순, 깻잎을 담고 썰어놓은 고기를 가지런히 담아 두 가지 소스와 함께 상에 냅니다. 원하는 채소에 고기와 당근, 무순을 올리고 소스를 넣어 드시면 됩니다.

Pork Belly Lettuce Wraps Dwehji Bossam

돼지 보쌈

Miso Pork Mac Jeok

맥적

4 Servings

1 lb.	Pork shoulder
As needed	Grapeseed oil

Seasoning

2 Tbsp	Miso
1 Tbsp	Soy sauce
2 Tbsp	Water
2 Tbsp	Red wine
3 Tbsp	Sugar
1 tsp	Honey
1 tsp	Sesame oil
1 tsp	Garlic, minced
1 tsp	Ginger, minced
1 tsp	Fresh oregano, chopped
1 tsp	Fresh thyme, chopped
TT*	Salt, pepper

*TT : To Taste

Preparation

1 Combine meat seasoning ingredients in a large bowl.

2 Slice pork into 1/4-inch thick pieces and pound lightly with a tenderizing hammer. Add pork to meat seasoning and let marinate in refrigerator for 2~3 hours.

3 Heat grapeseed oil in a large pan over medium heat and cook pork until just before done. Finish pork over high heat on a grill for 3~4 minutes (If grill is unavailable, just continue cooking in pan).

4 Serve pork with steamed rice.

4 인분

450 g	돼지고기 목살
적당량	포도씨 오일

고기 양념

일본 된장 2 큰술, 간장 1 큰술, 물 2 큰술,
레드와인 2 큰술, 설탕 3 큰술, 꿀 1 작은술,
참기름 1 작은술, 다진 마늘 1 작은술,
다진 생강 1 작은술, 다진 오레가노 1 작은술,
다진 타임 1 작은술, 소금 · 후추 적당량

준비 과정

1 분량의 고기 양념 재료를 볼에 담아 한데 섞어둡니다.

2 돼지고기 목살은 0.5cm 두께의 스테이크 모양으로 잘라 두드리는 기구로 살짝 두드려 준비된 양념에 재서 2~3시간 정도 냉장고에 둡니다.

3 프라이팬에 포도씨 오일을 두르고 고기를 올려 거의 다 익을 때까지 구워낸 후 뜨겁게 달궈진 그릴판 위에 한 번 더 올려 3~4분 정도 구워냅니다 (그릴판이 없으면 그냥 팬에서만 구워도 됩니다).

4 따뜻한 밥과 함께 상에 냅니다.

Thyme 타임

Oregano 오레가노

Grilled Spicy Pork Belly
삼겹살 고추장 구이

4 Servings

1 ½ lb.	Pork belly, cut into 1/4-inch thick pieces
1	Medium onion, sliced

Seasoning

2 Tbsp	Soy sauce
4 Tbsp	Red pepper paste
1 Tbsp	Dried red pepper powder
2 Tbsp	Sugar
1 Tbsp	Honey
2 Tbsp	Red wine
2 Tbsp	Onion, pureed
3 Tbsp	Scallion, chopped
1 Tbsp	Garlic, minced
1/2 Tbsp	Ginger, minced
1 Tbsp	Sesame oil
2 Tbsp	Sesame seeds
1/2 tsp	Pepper
TT*	Salt

*TT : To Taste

Preparation

1 Combine seasoning ingredients in a large bowl.

2 Add pork belly and let marinate in refrigerator for at least 1 hour.

3 Sauté pork belly in a large pan over medium-high heat. Add sliced onion about halfway through.

4 Serve with steamed rice.

Tip Red pepper paste brands have varying sugar content, so add more or less sugar as needed.

4 인분

675 g	두께 0.5cm로 썬 삼겹살
1 개분	저며 썬 중간 크기 양파

고추장 양념

간장 2 큰술, 고추장 4 큰술, 고춧가루 1 큰술, 설탕 2 큰술, 꿀 1 큰술, 레드와인 2 큰술, 양파즙 2 큰술, 다진 파 3 큰술, 다진 마늘 1 큰술, 다진 생강 1/2 큰술, 참기름 1 큰술, 참깨 2 큰술, 후추 1/2 작은술, 소금 적당량

준비 과정

1 고추장 양념 재료를 볼에 넣어 한데 섞어 둡니다.

2 섞어둔 양념에 삼겹살을 넣어 한 시간가량 냉장고에 넣고 재둡니다.

3 뜨거운 팬에 삼겹살을 넣고 앞뒤가 타지 않게 뒤집어가며 익히다 거의 다 익었을 때 양파를 넣고 고기가 완전히 다 익을 때까지 같이 볶아냅니다.

4 따뜻한 밥과 함께 상에 냅니다.

Tip 고추장에 따라 단맛이 다르니 설탕의 양을 조금씩 조절해 줍니다.

Baby Back Ribs
돼지갈비 찜

4 Servings

2 lb.	Baby back ribs
2 Tbsp	Pine nuts, chopped
2 Tbsp	Parsley, chopped

Seasoning

6 Tbsp	Soy sauce
6 Tbsp	Water
3 Tbsp	Sugar
2 Tbsp	Corn syrup
2 Tbsp	Red wine
2 Tbsp	Onion, pureed
4 Tbsp	Scallion, chopped
1½ Tbsp	Garlic, minced
1 Tbsp	Ginger, minced
1 Tbsp	Dried thyme, chopped
1 Tbsp	Sesame oil
1 Tbsp	Sesame seeds
1/2 Tbsp	Pepper

Preparation

1 Combine seasoning ingredients in a large bowl.

2 Rinse baby back ribs and pat dry with paper towel. Combine ribs with seasoning and let marinate for 1 hour.

3 Place ribs and sauce in a large pot and cook over medium heat for 40~50 minutes, stirring occasionally.

4 Serve garnished with chopped pine nuts and parsley.

4 인분

900 g	돼지갈비
2 큰술	잣가루
2 큰술	다진 파슬리

돼지갈비 양념

간장 6 큰술, 물 6 큰술, 설탕 3 큰술,
물엿이나 시럽 2 큰술, 레드와인 2 큰술, 양파즙 2 큰술,
다진 파 4 큰술, 다진 마늘 1½ 큰술, 다진 생강 1 큰술,
다진 말린 타임 1 큰술, 참기름 1 큰술, 참깨 1 큰술,
후추 1/2 큰술

준비 과정

1 돼지갈비 양념 재료를 볼에 넣어 한데 섞어둡니다.

2 돼지갈비는 깨끗이 씻어 준비된 양념에 1시간 정도 버무려 둡니다.

3 큰 냄비에 양념에 버무린 돼지갈비를 넣고 끓입니다. 돼지갈비가 끓으면 중불로 줄여 소스가 다 졸아들 때까지 40~50분 정도 끓입니다. 중간중간 한 번씩 돼지갈비와 소스를 저어줍니다.

4 접시에 담고 잣가루와 파슬리를 뿌려 상에 냅니다.

Ginger Soy Fried Baby Back Ribs

돼지갈비 튀김

4 Servings

5 lb.	Baby back ribs
1 lb.	Corn starch
30~40 oz.	Canola oil
As needed	Parsley
As needed	Spring salad mix

Seasoning

1 cup	Soy sauce
1 cup	Sugar
3 Tbsp	Sesame oil
3 Tbsp	Garlic, minced
6 Tbsp	Ginger, minced
3 Tbsp	Sesame seeds
4 Tbsp	Water

Preparation

1 Combine seasoning ingredients in a large bowl.

2 Soak ribs in water for 30 minutes. Remove and blot dry with paper towel. Add ribs to seasoning and let marinate in refrigerator for at least 3~4 hours.

3 Fill a wok or large pot halfway up with canola oil and bring to 350°F.

4 Dredge ribs in corn starch and shake off excess. Carefully place ribs in oil and deep-fry ribs until golden brown.

5 Garnish ribs with chopped parsely and serve with spring salad mix.

4 인분

2,25 kg	돼지갈비
450 g	녹말가루
4~6 컵	카놀라 오일
적당량	파슬리
적당량	샐러드 믹스

소스

간장 1 컵, 설탕 1 컵, 참기름 3 큰술, 다진 마늘 3 큰술, 다진 생강 6 큰술, 참깨 3 큰술, 물 4 큰술

준비 과정

1 돼지갈비 소스를 볼에 담아 한데 섞어둡니다.

2 돼지갈비는 물에 30분간 담가 핏물을 빼고 물기가 없게 닦아준 뒤 준비된 소스에 넣고 3~4시간 정도 냉장고에 재둡니다.

3 웍이나 깊이가 깊은 프라이팬에 카놀라 오일을 절반 정도 넣고 기름의 온도를 175℃로 준비합니다.

4 돼지갈비에 녹말가루를 골고루 묻혀 가루를 털어낸 후, 녹말가루를 묻힌 돼지갈비를 넣어 튀깁니다. 껍질이 바삭하도록 두 번 튀겨서 건져 종이타월에 올려 기름을 뺍니다.

5 튀긴 돼지갈비와 샐러드 믹스를 접시에 담고 파슬리로 모양을 내 상에 냅니다.

Sweet and Sour Pork Tahngsooyook

탕수육

4 Servings

1 lb.	Pork loin, cut into bite-sized pieces
2 Tbsp	Soy sauce
1 Tbsp	Red wine
1	Pineapple
As needed	Olive oil, canola oil

Sauce

1 ½ cup	Water
6 Tbsp	Sugar
6 Tbsp	Vinegar
1 Tbsp	Pineapple juice
1 Tbsp	Soy sauce
1tsp	Salt
4 Tbsp	Corn starch/water mixture (1:2 ratio)
1	Onion, sliced
1	Cucumber, sliced thin
1/2	Carrot, sliced thin
2	Dried shitake mushrooms, soaked, sliced
1 slice	Pineapple, cut in cubes

Batter

1 cup	Corn starch
1/4 cup	Water
1	Egg
1 tsp	Salt, sugar

Preparation

1 Cut pineapple in half lengthwise and scoop out a large opening. Set aside in refrigerator.

2 Combine pork loin, soy sauce, and red wine and let marinate for 20 minutes.

3 Bring a small pot of water, sugar, vinegar, pineapple juice, soy sauce and salt to a boil. Add corn starch/water mixture and boil for a few more minutes. Remove from heat.

4 Heat olive oil in a pan over medium heat and sauté sliced onion until soft. Add cucumber, carrot, mushrooms, and pineapple cubes cook for a few more minutes. Pour pineapple soy mixture into the pan and mix well. Remove from heat and set aside.

5 Combine batter ingredients in a large bowl.

6 Fill a wok or large pot halfway up with canola oil and bring to 350°F. Coat pork loin with batter and deep-fry until golden brown and crispy.

7 Toss fried pork loin in sauce and serve in scooped out pinepple.

Tip Do not coat fried pork loin too heavily in sauce. Toss lightly and serve remainder of sauce on the side.

4 인분

450 g	먹기 좋은 크기로 썬 돼지고기 살코기
2 큰술	간장
1 큰술	레드와인
1 개	파인애플
적당량	올리브오일, 카놀라 오일

소스

물 1 ½ 컵, 설탕 6 큰술, 식초 6 큰술,
파인애플 주스 1 큰술, 간장 1 큰술, 소금 1 작은술,
녹말물 4 큰술 (녹말과 물의 비율 1 : 2), 썬 양파 1 개분,
가늘게 썬 오이 1 개분, 가늘게 썬 당근 1/2개분,
썬 표고버섯 2 개분, 깍둑 썬 파인애플 1 쪽분

튀김 반죽

녹말가루 1 컵, 물 1/4 컵, 달걀 1 개, 소금·설탕 적당량

준비 과정

1 파인애플을 가로로 잘라낸 후 속을 파서 준비해 놓습니다.

2 돼지고기는 살코기로 준비해 간장과 레드와인에 20분 정도 재둡니다.

3 냄비에 물, 설탕, 식초, 파인애플 주스, 간장, 소금을 넣고 끓여 소스를 만듭니다. 끓으면 녹말물을 부어 조금 더 끓이다 불을 끕니다.

4 중불 프라이팬에 올리브오일을 두르고 양파를 볶다가 잘게 썬 오이, 당근, 불린 표고버섯, 파인애플을 넣어 잠시 더 볶습니다. 준비해 둔 소스를 넣고 섞어준 후 불을 끕니다.

5 녹말가루와 물, 달걀, 소금, 설탕을 잘 섞어 튀김 반죽을 준비합니다.

6 양념된 돼지고기에 반죽을 잘 묻힌 후, 175 ℃의 카놀라 오일에 두 번 튀겨냅니다.

7 튀긴 고기를 파인애플 껍질 안에 넣고 소스를 끼얹어 상에 냅니다.

Tip 튀긴 돼지고기에 탕수육 소스를 너무 많이 묻히지 말고 살짝 끼얹은 후 나머지 소스는 볼에 담아 같이 상에 냅니다.

Fried Pork Cutlet Donkasu
돈가스

4 Servings

1 lb.	Pork chops
2 cups	Flour
2	Eggs, whipped (egg wash)
2 cup	Bread crumbs
1/4	Cabbage, sliced thin
As needed	Vegetable oil
TT *	Salt, pepper

Sauce

3 Tbsp	Teriyaki sauce
1 Tbsp	Worcestershire sauce
1 Tbsp	Lemon juice
1/2 tsp	Sugar
TT *	Pepper

Dressing for Cabbage

4 Tbsp	Mayonnaise
2 Tbsp	Ketchup
1 Tbsp	Lemon juice
1 Tbsp	Parsley, chopped
1 tsp	Sugar
TT *	Salt

* TT : To Taste

Preparation

1 Combine sauce and dressing ingredients in separate bowls. Set aside.

2 Pound pork chops with a tenderizing hammer until thin and uniform. Season with salt and pepper.

3 Dredge pork chops in flour and shake off excess. Dip pork chops in egg wash and toss in bread crumbs.

4 Fill a wok or large pot halfway up with vegetable oil and bring to 350°F. Add pork chops and deep-fry until golden brown. Remove pork cutlet and place on paper towel to allow oil to drain.

5 Lightly drizzle sauce over pork cutlet, toss cabbage in dressing, and serve with remainder of sauce on the side.

4 인분

450 g	얇게 썬 돼지고기
2 컵	밀가루
2 개	달걀
2 컵	빵가루
1/4 개분	얇게 썬 양배추
적당량	식용유
적당량	소금, 후추

찍어 먹는 소스
데리야키 소스 3 큰술, 우스터 소스 1 큰술, 레몬즙 1 큰술,
설탕 1/2 작은술, 후추 적당량

양배추 드레싱
마요네즈 4 큰술, 토마토케첩 2 큰술, 레몬즙 1큰술,
다진 파슬리 1 큰술, 설탕 1 작은술, 소금 적당량

준비 과정

1 찍어 먹는 소스와 양배추 드레싱 재료를 각각 다른 볼에 넣고 섞어 준비합니다.

2 돼지고기는 두드리는 기구로 앞뒤를 살짝 더 두드려 준 후 소금과 후추 간을 해둡니다.

3 돼지고기에 밀가루를 살짝 묻혀 털어낸 후 달걀물이 골고루 묻도록 뒤적거려서 빵가루를 묻힙니다. 기름에 넣기 바로 전에 준비합니다.

4 웍이나 오목한 팬에 식용유를 절반쯤 붓고 기름이 175℃가 되게 끓인 후 돼지고기가 노릇노릇해질 때까지 튀깁니다. 더 바삭하게 되도록 한 번 더 튀겨준 후 종이타월에 놓고 기름을 뺍니다.

5 돈가스에 찍어 먹는 소스를 살짝 뿌리고, 양배추는 드레싱에 잘 버무려 상에 냅니다. 찍어 먹는 소스와 양배추 드레싱은 돈가스와 함께 상에 냅니다.

Tofu with Kimchi and Pork Belly
두부 김치 두루치기

4 Servings

1 pack	Tofu, cut into 1/2-inch thick squares
12 oz.	Pork belly, bacon sliced
1 lb.	Ripe kimchi
1 Tbsp	Butter
1/2	Onion, sliced
1	Red pepper, cut diagonally
4 Tbsp	Scallion, chopped
As needed	Vegetable oil

Seasoning

1 Tbsp	Soy sauce
1 Tbsp	Dried red pepper powder
1 Tbsp	Red pepper paste
1 Tbsp	Sugar
1 tsp	Garlic, minced
1/2 tsp	Ginger, minced
1/2 Tbsp	Sesame seeds
1/2 Tbsp	Sesame oil

Preparation

1 Cut pork belly and kimchi into $1\frac{1}{2}$-inch long pieces. Combine pork and kimchi with seasoning ingredients in a large bowl and let marinate in refrigerator for at least 1 hour.

2 Season both sides of tofu with salt. Heat vegetable oil in a large pan over medium-high heat. Add tofu and sauté until both sides are golden brown. Remove and set aside under foil to keep warm.

3 Melt butter in a large pan over medium-high heat and sauté onions until soft. Add pork belly and kimchi until pork is done. Add scallions and red pepper, turn off heat, and stir for another minute.

4 Arrange tofu around kimchi and pork belly and serve.

4 인분

1 팩	두부
350 g	돼지고기 삼겹살
450 g	잘 익은 김치
1 큰술	버터
1/2 개	잘게 썬 양파
1 개	어슷하게 썬 홍고추
4 큰술	다진 파
적당량	식용유

양념

간장 1 큰술, 고춧가루 1 큰술, 고추장 1 큰술, 설탕 1 큰술, 다진 마늘 1 작은술, 다진 생강 1/2 작은술, 참깨 1/2 큰술, 참기름 1/2 큰술

준비 과정

1 돼지고기와 김치는 4cm 길이로 썰어 분량의 양념에 재서 1시간 정도 냉장고에 둡니다.

2 두부는 앞뒤로 소금을 뿌려 식용유를 두른 중불 프라이팬에 노릇노릇하게 지져냅니다. 두부를 꺼낸 후 식지 않도록 호일을 덮어둡니다.

3 프라이팬에 버터를 두르고 양파를 볶다가 고기와 김치를 넣고 고기가 다 익을 때까지 볶습니다. 다 익은 듯하면 파와 홍고추를 섞고 불을 끕니다.

4 김치와 돼지고기 볶은 것을 가운데 놓고 준비된 두부를 가장자리에 둘러 상에 냅니다.

Soy Ginger Chicken Drummettes
Dahk Gangjung 닭강정

4 Servings

2½ lb.	Chicken drummettes (about 20 pieces)
TT*	Salt, pepper
1/2	Lemon, juiced
1 cup	Corn starch
As needed	Canola oil

Sauce

5 Tbsp	Soy sauce
3 Tbsp	Sugar
2 Tbsp	Corn syrup
1 Tbsp	Garlic, minced
1 Tbsp	Ginger, minced
1 Tbsp	Sesame oil
1 tsp	Salt
8 Tbsp	Water
TT*	Pepper

* TT : To Taste

Preparation

1 Marinate chicken drummettes with salt, pepper, and lemon juice for at least 1 hour.

2 Fill a wok or large pot halfway up with oil and bring to 375°F.

3 Dredge drummettes in corn starch and shake off excess. Carefully place drummettes in oil (do not overfill) and deep-fry until golden brown.

4 Combine sauce ingredients in a large pan and simmer over low heat. Add drummettes and toss in sauce. Serve immediately.

4 인분

1.2 kg	닭봉 (20개 정도)
적당량	소금, 후추
1/2 개	레몬
적당량	카놀라 오일
1 컵	녹말가루

소스

간장 5 큰술, 설탕 3 큰술, 물엿이나 시럽 2 큰술,
다진 마늘 1 큰술, 다진 생강 1 큰술, 참기름 1 큰술,
소금 1 작은술, 물 8 큰술, 후추 적당량

준비 과정

1 닭봉을 소금, 후추, 레몬즙에 버무려 한 시간 정도 재둡니다.

2 웍이나 오목한 프라이팬에 카놀라 오일을 넣고 기름의 온도가 190℃가 되도록 달궈줍니다.

3 닭봉에 녹말가루를 묻히고 가루를 털어낸 후 끓는 기름에 한 번 튀겨내고 더 바삭하게 다시 한 번 더 튀깁니다(튀김을 할 때 기름이 뜨겁게 유지되도록 한 번에 닭봉 6~7개씩만 집어넣어 튀깁니다).

4 얕은 냄비나 큰 프라이팬에 양념 소스 재료를 넣고 양념이 약간 졸아들도록 끓이다가 튀겨낸 닭을 넣고 양념에 잘 섞어줍니다. 뜨거울 때 접시에 담아 상에 냅니다.

Con
1 cer
1 salt
1 1/2
cabb
1 1/2
(tang
3 table
1 large
2 table
2 squar
halved
1/2 cup
with p

1 Put the chicken st
oil. Lower heat, cc
bout 15 minutes. R
Add the rice to th
aucepan and simm
o and the stock re
bowls, then add th
d pepper to each
While the rice is co
all bowls and serv

te: To make crisp
t until golden bro
drain on paper t
t Asian stores se
erved black bear
able in plastic p

Oregano Chicken
오레가노 향이 나는 닭다리 찜

4 Servings

12	Large chicken legs
TT*	Salt, pepper
1	Lemon, juiced
1/2 stalk	Leek, chopped
1 cup	Chicken stock
As needed	Olive oil

Sauce

1	Apple, pureed
1/2	Onion, pureed
7 Tbsp	Soy sauce
1 Tbsp	Garlic, minced
1 tsp	Ginger, minced
4 Tbsp	Sugar
1 tsp	Salt
3 Tbsp	Fresh oregano, chopped
TT*	Pepper

*TT : To Taste

Preparation

1 Combine sauce ingredients in a large bowl.

2 Season chicken legs with salt, pepper, and lemon juice. Add chicken to sauce and let marinate in refrigerator for at least 30 minutes.

3 Heat olive oil in a large pan over high heat. Add chicken and leeks and cook until chicken is golden brown. Add chicken stock and cover until chicken is cooked through.

4 Serve chicken legs with steamed rice.

Tip Dried oregano can be substituted for fresh oregano.

---

4 인분

12 개	큰 닭다리
적당량	소금, 후추
1 개	레몬즙
1/2 줄기	다진 대파
1 컵	닭 육수
적당량	올리브오일

양념

사과즙 1 개분, 양파즙 1/2 개분, 간장 7 큰술,
다진 마늘 1 큰술, 다진 생강 1 작은술, 설탕 4 큰술,
소금 1 작은술, 다진 프레시 오레가노 3 큰술, 후추 적당량

준비 과정

1 소스 재료를 볼에 한데 섞어둡니다.

2 닭다리는 깨끗이 씻어 소금, 후추, 레몬을 뿌린 후 준비된 소스에 버무려 30분 정도 재둡니다.

3 달궈진 프라이팬에 올리브오일을 두르고 닭다리를 앞뒤로 노릇노릇하게 지지다가 대파를 넣고 잠시 볶은 후 닭 육수를 붓고 닭다리가 완전히 익을 때까지 뚜껑을 덮어둡니다.

4 접시에 익은 닭다리를 담고 따뜻한 밥과 함께 상에 냅니다.

Tip 프레시 오레가노가 없으면 병에 든 말린 오레가노를 사용합니다.

Oregano 오레가노

Spicy Chicken and Potato Dahk Doritang

닭도리탕

4 Servings

2 lb.	Whole chicken, cut into pieces
2	Idaho potatoes, cut into 2-inch pieces
1 cup	Chicken stock
As needed	Olive oil

Seasoning

1 Tbsp	Soy sauce
5 Tbsp	Red pepper paste
1 Tbsp	Dried red pepper powder
1 Tbsp	Garlic, minced
1 tsp	Ginger, minced
1 Tbsp	Sugar
1 Tbsp	Sesame oil
1 Tbsp	Sesame seeds
1/2 tsp	Salt
1/2 tsp	Pepper

Preparation

1 Combine seasoning ingredients in a large bowl.

2 Add chicken and let marinate for 30 minutes.

3 Heat olive oil in a large pot over medium heat. Add chicken and sauté for 5 minutes. Add chicken stock and bring to a boil.

4 Add potato and simmer over medium heat for an additional 30 minutes. Stir occasionally.

5 Serve with steamed rice.

Tip Red pepper paste brands have varying sugar content, so add more or less sugar as needed.

4 인분

900 g	토막 낸 닭
2 개분	5cm 정도로 썬 감자
1 컵	닭 육수
적당량	올리브오일

양념

간장 1 큰술, 고추장 5 큰술, 고춧가루 1큰술,
다진 마늘 1 큰술, 다진 생강 1 작은술, 설탕 1큰술,
참기름 1큰술, 참깨 1 큰술, 소금 1/2 작은술,
후추 1/2 작은술

준비 과정

1 분량의 양념을 한데 섞어둡니다.

2 닭은 양념에 30분 동안 재둡니다.

3 큰 냄비에 양념된 닭을 넣고 5분 정도 볶다가 닭 육수를 붓고 끓입니다.

4 감자를 넣고 중불에서 한 번씩 저어주며 30분간 양념이 졸아들도록 끓입니다.

5 따뜻한 밥과 함께 상에 냅니다.

Tip 고추장에 따라 조금씩 맛이 다르니 설탕은 적당량 조절하면 됩니다.

Spicy Chicken Stir Fry with Vegetables
Dahk Galbi 닭갈비

4 Servings

1 1/2 lb.	Chicken thigh, boneless and skinless
1	Korean yam, sliced diagonally
1	Onion, sliced
1/4	Cabbage, julienned
5	Sesame leaves, julienned
1 stalk	Scallion, cut diagonally
As needed	Olive oil
1/2 cup	Rice cake, sliced thin, soaked (optional)

Seasoning

2 Tbsp	Soy sauce
2 Tbsp	Red pepper paste
2 Tbsp	Dried red pepper powder
1 Tbsp	Garlic, minced
1 tsp	Ginger, minced
1 Tbsp	Sesame oil
2 Tbsp	White wine
1 Tbsp	Sugar
1 Tbsp	Honey
1 Tbsp	Curry powder
1 Tbsp	Sesame seeds
1 tsp	Salt
TT*	Salt, pepper

*TT : To Taste

Preparation

1 Combine seasoning ingredients in a large bowl.

2 Rinse chicken and blot dry with paper towel. Cut into bite-sized pieces and combine with seasoning. Cover and let marinate in refrigerator for 1~2 hours.

3 Heat olive oil in a large pan over medium-high heat and add yam and sliced onion. When onions become soft, add chicken and cabbage and cook for another 20 minutes. Add sesame leaves and scallion when chicken is almost done.

4 Rice cakes can be added with chicken and cabbage.

5 Serve with steamed rice.

Tip Add steamed rice, red pepper paste, and sesame oil to leftovers to create a fantastic fried rice.

Korean yam 고구마

Sesame seed leaves 깻잎

4 인분

675 g	껍질 벗긴 뼈 없는 닭고기
1 개분	어슷 썬 고구마
1 개분	썬 양파
1/4 개분	가늘게 길이로 썬 양배추
5 장분	가늘게 길이로 썬 깻잎
1 줄기	어슷 썬 파
적당량	올리브오일
1/2 컵	불린 떡국 떡 (선택)

양념

간장 2 큰술, 고추장 2 큰술, 고춧가루 2 큰술,
다진 마늘 1 큰술, 다진 생강 1 작은술, 참기름 1 큰술,
화이트와인 2 큰술, 설탕 1 큰술, 꿀 1 큰술,
카레가루 1 큰술, 참깨 1 큰술, 소금 1 작은술,
소금 · 후추 적당량

준비 과정

1 양념을 큰 볼에 잘 섞어둡니다.

2 닭고기를 잘 씻어 물기를 닦은 후 먹기 좋은 크기로 잘라 준비된 양념에 재서 1~2시간 정도 냉장고에 넣어 둡니다.

3 넓은 프라이팬에 올리브오일을 넉넉히 두른 후 얇게 썬 고구마를 밑에 깔고 양파를 넣어 먼저 익힙니다. 양파가 많이 익었을 때 닭고기, 양배추를 넣고, 20분 정도 후 닭고기가 거의 다 익었을 때 깻잎과 파를 넣습니다.

4 떡국 떡이 있으면 물에 불려 준비했다가 닭고기와 양배추를 넣을 때 함께 넣어주면 됩니다.

5 큰 그릇에 담아 따뜻한 밥과 함께 상에 냅니다.

Tip 고기와 야채가 조금 남았을 때 밥, 고추장, 참기름을 넣어 볶아 드시면 맛있습니다.

Mango Teriyaki Chicken
망고 소스를 곁들인 데리야키 치킨

4 Servings

1½ lb.	Chicken breast
TT*	Salt, pepper

Teriyaki Sauce

4 Tbsp	Soy sauce
4 Tbsp	Mirin
4 Tbsp	Sugar
4 Tbsp	Water
1 Tbsp	Garlic, minced
1 tsp	Ginger, minced

Mango Sauce

2 Tbsp	Shallot, chopped
2 Tbsp	Parsley, chopped
1 Tbsp	Teriyaki sauce
1/2 cup	White wine
2 Tbsp	Heavy cream
1/2 cup	Chicken stock
1	Mango, diced
1 tsp	Salt
TT*	Pepper

*TT : To Taste

Preparation

1 Combine teriyaki sauce ingredients in a medium-sized pan and bring to a boil. Reduce heat and let simmer for 5 minutes.

2 Season chicken breast with salt and pepper and marinate chicken in 6 tablespoons of sauce for at least 1 hour.

3 Fry chicken in a large pan over medium heat with olive oil until cooked through. Remove and set aside.

4 In the same pan, sauté shallots until soft. Add parsley, 1 tablespoon of teriyaki sauce, white wine, heavy cream, and chicken stock. Once the mixture reaches a boil, add mango and cook for another 2~3 minutes.

5 Pour mango sauce over the chicken and serve garnished with diced mango and parsley.

Tip Onion can be substituted for shallot.

---

4 인분

680 g	닭가슴살
적당량	소금, 후추

데리야키 소스
간장 4 큰술, 맛술 4 큰술, 설탕 4 큰술, 물 4 큰술,
다진 마늘 1 큰술, 다진 생강 1 작은술

망고 소스
다진 샬롯(양파) 2 큰술, 다진 파슬리 2 큰술,
데리야키 소스 1 큰술,화이트와인 1/2 컵, 생크림 2 큰술,
닭 육수 1/2 컵, 작게 깍둑 썬 망고 1 개분, 소금 1 작은술,
후추 적당량

준비 과정

1 데리야키 소스 재료를 작은 냄비에 담고 한소끔 끓이다 불을 줄여서 5분 정도 끓인 후 불을 끄고 식힙니다.

2 닭은 소금과 후추로 간을 한 후 데리야키 소스 6큰술을 넣고 섞어 한 시간 가량 재둡니다.

3 중불 프라이팬에 올리브오일을 두르고 닭가슴살을 앞뒤로 지져 접시에 꺼내 놓습니다. 그릴에 구우면 더욱 좋습니다.

4 닭을 지진 팬에 샬롯을 볶다가 샬롯이 반쯤 익으면, 파슬리와 데리야키 소스 1큰술, 화이트와인, 생크림, 닭 육수를 넣고 끓입니다. 한 번 끓으면 망고를 넣고 2~3분 더 끓여 소스를 만듭니다.

5 접시에 올려 놓은 닭가슴살 위에 망고 소스를 끼얹고, 깍둑 썬 망고와 파슬리로 장식해 상에 냅니다.

Tip[1] 시중에 파는 데리야키 소스를 사용하면 편리합니다.
  [2] 샬롯이 없으면 양파를 사용합니다.

Spicy Scallops
매운 소스를 곁들인 관자구이

4 Servings

8	Large scallops
TT*	Salt, pepper
1	Lemon juice
2 Tbsp	Parsley, chopped
As needed	Olive oil

Sauce

1 Tbsp	Shallot, chopped fine
2 Tbsp	Japanese mayonnaise
1 tsp	Hichimi
1 tsp	Chili sauce, La Yu, or hot sauce
1 tsp	Truffle oil (optional)
1 tsp	Water
1/2 tsp	Sugar
1/2 tsp	Garlic powder
TT*	Salt, pepper

*TT : To Taste

Preparation

1 Combine sauce ingredients in a small bowl. Set aside.

2 Blot dry scallops with paper towel and season with salt, pepper, and lemon juice.

3 Grill or pan fry scallops over high heat until desired doneness (take care not to overcook scallops).

4 Drizzle scallops with hot sauce and serve garnished with chopped parsley.

4 인분

8개	관자 큰 것
적당량	소금, 후추
1 개분	레몬즙
2 큰술	다진 파슬리
적당량	올리브오일

매운 소스

곱게 다진 샬롯(양파) 1 큰술, 일본 마요네즈 2 큰술,
히치미 1 작은술, 칠리소스나 고추기름, 핫소스 1 작은술,
트러플 오일 (선택) 1 작은술, 물 1 작은술,
설탕 1/2 작은술, 마늘가루 1/2 작은술

준비 과정

1 매운 소스 재료를 한데 섞어둡니다.

2 관자를 깨끗이 씻어 종이타월로 잘 닦은 후 소금, 후추와 레몬즙을 뿌려둡니다.

3 뜨겁게 달궈진 그릴이나 올리브오일을 두른 프라이팬에 관자를 올려 앞뒤로 너무 익지 않게 구워줍니다 (손으로 눌렀을 때 어느 정도 단단한 느낌이 나면 됩니다).

4 접시에 구운 관자를 담고 준비된 매운 소스를 가늘게 지그재그로 뿌린 후 다진 파슬리로 장식해 상에 냅니다.

Spicy Grilled Shrimp
머리 달린 매운 새우구이

4 Servings

8	Shrimp with head
1 pack	Spring salad mix
As needed	Olive oil

Sauce

1 Tbsp	Soy sauce
2 Tbsp	White wine
1 Tbsp	Chili sauce
2 Tbsp	Lemon juice
2 Tbsp	Orange juice
1 tsp	Garlic, minced
1/2 tsp	Ginger, minced
1 tsp	Sugar
1 tsp	Dried marjoram
TT*	Salt, pepper

*TT : To Taste

Preparation

1 Combine sauce ingredients in a medium-sized bowl.

2 Cut shrimp in half and combine with sauce. Let marinate in refrigerator overnight.

3 Grill or pan fry shrimp over high heat until fully cooked.

4 Arrange shrimp over spring salad mix and serve.

Tip Other herbs can be substituted for marjoram.

---

4 인분

8마리	머리 달린 새우
1 팩	샐러드 믹스
적당량	올리브오일

양념

간장 1 큰술, 화이트와인 2 큰술, 칠리 페이스트 1 큰술,
레몬즙 2 큰술, 오렌지주스 2 큰술, 다진 마늘 1 작은술,
다진 생강 1/2 작은술, 설탕 1 작은술,
말린 마조램 1 작은술, 소금 · 후추 적당량

준비 과정

1 분량의 양념을 볼에 잘 섞어둡니다.

2 새우를 잘 씻은 후 반으로 잘라 양념과 잘 섞어 냉장고에 하루 밤 동안 재둡니다.

3 뜨겁게 달궈진 그릴에 새우가 앞뒤로 잘 익도록 구워냅니다 (그릴이 없으면 프라이팬에 구워냅니다).

4 구운 새우를 샐러드 믹스와 함께 상에 냅니다.

Tip 마조램을 구하기 힘들면 좋아하는 허브로 대신해도 됩니다.

Shrimp with Broccoli

브로콜리를 곁들인 새우볶음

4 Servings

1 lb	Medium-sized shrimp
10 oz.	Broccoli
As needed	Olive oil

Sauce
5 Tbsp	Glazed Teriyaki sauce
3 Tbsp	Ketchup
2 Tbsp	Garlic, minced
1 tsp	Ginger, minced
1 Tbsp	Tabasco sauce
1/2 Tbsp	Sugar
2 Tbsp	Water
TT*	Salt, pepper

*TT : To Taste

Preparation

1 Combine sauce ingredients in a medium-sized bowl.

2 Bring a large pot of salt water to a boil and blanch broccoli.

3 De-vein shrimp, leaving the shell intact, and rinse.

4 Heat olive oil in a large fryng pan over high heat and add shrimp and 2/3 of the sauce. Cook until shrimp just turns color.

5 Add broccoli and remaining sauce and cook until shrimp is cooked through.

6 Serve while hot.

Tip Cauliflower can be substituted for broccoli.

4 인분

450 g (15~17마리)	중간 크기 새우
285 g	브로콜리
적당량	올리브오일

소스

데리야키 소스 5 큰술, 토마토케첩 3 큰술,
다진 마늘 2 큰술, 다진 생강 1 작은술, 타바스코 소스 1 큰술,
설탕 1/2 큰술, 물 2 큰술, 소금 · 후추 적당량

준비 과정

1 소스 재료를 볼에 넣어 한데 섞어둡니다.

2 브로콜리를 뜨거운 물에 살짝 데친 후 찬물에 씻어 물기를 빼놓습니다.

3 새우는 등 쪽으로 가위를 넣어 갈라서 까만 내장을 빼내고 깨끗이 씻은 다음 껍질과 꼬리를 그대로 남겨둡니다.

4 뜨거운 프라이팬에 준비된 소스를 2/3 정도 넣고, 새우가 오렌지색이 돌 때까지 볶습니다.

5 데쳐 놓은 브로콜리를 넣고 남은 1/3 의 소스를 모두 넣은 후 새우가 다 익을 때까지 볶아줍니다.

6 뜨거울 때 드셔야 좋습니다.

Tip 브로콜리 대신 콜리플라워를 섞어 사용해도 좋습니다.

Fried Shrimp and Squid

새우와 오징어 튀김

4 Servings

1 lb.	Squid, body only
1 lb	Large shrimp
1	Lemon, juiced
1 cup	Tempura batter mix
2 cup	Panko
TT*	Salt
As needed	Vegetable oil

Dipping Sauce

1 Tbsp	Soy sauce
1/2 Tbsp	Vinegar
1/2 Tbsp	Lemon juice
1/2 tsp	Sugar
1 Tbsp	Scallion, chopped
1 Tbsp	Sesame seeds

*TT : To Taste

Preparation

1 Combine dipping sauce ingredients in a small bowl. Set aside.

2 Cut squid into 1/2-inch thick rings. Season squid and shrimp with lemon juice.

3 Combine tempura batter mix, ice cold water, and a pinch of salt in a medium-sized bowl.

4 Fill a wok or large pot halfway up with vegetable oil and bring to 375°F. Coat squid with tempura batter and shake off excess. Add squid to wok and fry until golden brown. Remove squid and place on paper towel. Season with salt while still hot.

5 Coat shrimp with tempura batter and shake off excess. Coat with panko and fry until golden brown. Remove shrimp and place on paper towel. Season with salt while still hot.

6 Serve shrimp and squid with dipping sauce.

Tip This recipe works great with vegetables as well.

4 인분

450 g	오징어
450 g (16~20 마리)	큰 새우
1 개	레몬
1 컵	튀김가루
2 컵	빵가루
적당량	소금
적당량	식용유

소스

간장 1 큰술, 식초 1/2 큰술, 레몬즙 1/2 큰술,
설탕 1/2 작은술, 다진 파 1 큰술, 참깨 1 큰술

준비 과정

1 찍어 먹는 소스 재료를 한데 섞어둡니다.

2 오징어는 몸통 부분만 씁니다. 깨끗이 씻은 오징어는 동그란 모양이 나오도록 1cm 간격으로 썰어 레몬 반쪽을 잘라 뿌립니다. 새우도 레몬을 뿌려둡니다.

3 튀김가루를 찬물에 걸쭉하게 개서 소금을 조금 넣어 준비합니다.

4 종이타월로 오징어 물기를 닦아서 튀김 반죽에 넣었다 뺀 후 190℃로 달궈진 식용유에 노릇노릇해질 때까지 튀깁니다. 더 바삭한 튀김을 위해 한 번 더 튀긴 후 종이타월에 놓고 기름을 뺄 때 소금을 살짝 뿌려줍니다.

5 새우도 종이타월로 물기를 닦아서 튀김 반죽에 넣었다 뺀 후 빵가루를 묻혀 오징어 튀김과 같은 방법으로 튀겨줍니다.

6 튀긴 새우와 오징어를 접시에 담고 찍어 먹는 소스와 함께 상에 냅니다.

Tip 좋아하는 채소를 썰어 튀겨 함께 내도 좋습니다.

Stir Fry Spicy Squid Ojinguh Bokum
오징어 볶음

4 Servings

1 lb.	Squid, body only
1	Medium onion, sliced
1	Carrot, cut into 2-inch long strips
1	Large green onion, cut into 2-inch long strips
2	Scallion, cut into 2-inch long strips
1	Green pepper, cut diagonally
1	Red pepper, cut diagonally
As needed	Oilive oil

Seasoning

2 Tbsp	Soy sauce
2 Tbsp	Red pepper paste
3 Tbsp	Dried red pepper powder
1 Tbsp	Garlic, minced
1/2 tsp	Ginger, minced
1 Tbsp	Sugar
1 Tbsp	Sesame oil
1 Tbsp	Sesame seeds
1 tsp	Salt
TT*	Pepper

*TT : To Taste

Preparation

1 Combine seasoning ingredients in a large bowl.

2 Blot dry squid with paper towel. Lightly score squid lengthwise and crosswise and cut into 2-inch thick strips.

3 Heat olive oil in a large pan over medium-high heat and sauté squid for 2~3 minutes. Drain liquid from the pan. Add 1 tablespoon of seasoning and sauté for another minute. Remove and set aside. Wipe pan clean.

4 Heat oil in the same pan over medium-high heat and sauté onions, carrots, large green onion, and scallion with remaining seasoning for 4~5 minutes. Add squid, green pepper, and red pepper and sauté for another 2~3 minutes. Add a drizzle of sesame oil just before removing from heat.

5 Serve with steamed rice.

Tip Red pepper paste brands have varying sugar content, so add more or less sugar as needed.

4 인분

450 g	오징어 몸통 부분으로만
1 개분	채 썬 양파
1 개분	5cm 길이로 썬 당근
1 줄기분	5cm 길이로 썬 대파
2 줄기분	5cm 길이로 썬 파
1 개분	어슷 썬 풋고추
1 개분	어슷 썬 홍고추
적당량	올리브오일

양념
간장 2 큰술, 고추장 2 큰술, 고춧가루 3 큰술,
다진 마늘 1 큰술, 다진 생강 1/2 작은술, 설탕 1 큰술,
참기름 1 큰술, 참깨 1 큰술, 소금 1 작은술,
후추 적당량

준비 과정

1 양념을 한데 섞어둡니다.

2 깨끗이 씻은 오징어는 가늘게 가로세로 칼집을 넣은 후 5 cm 길이로 썰어 놓습니다.

3 뜨거운 팬에 올리브오일을 두르고 오징어를 2~3분 정도 살짝 볶아 물기를 따라내고 양념 1큰술을 넣고 뒤적여준 후 접시에 담아둡니다.

4 뜨거운 팬에 양파, 당근, 대파, 파와 나머지 양념을 넣고 4~5분 정도 볶다가 오징어와 풋고추, 홍고추를 넣고 2~3분 정도 같이 볶습니다. 꺼내기 직전 참기름을 약간 넣고 섞어줍니다.

5 따뜻한 밥과 함께 상에 냅니다.

Tip 고추장에 따라 단맛이 다르니 설탕의 양을 조절해 줍니다.

Grilled Mackerel

고등어구이

4 Servings

1½ lb.	Mackerel, filleted
1/2	Lemon, juiced
TT*	Salt
2 stalks	Scallion, julienned

Seasoning

3 Tbsp	Soy sauce
2 Tbsp	White wine
1 Tbsp	Sugar
1½ Tbsp	Ginger, minced

*TT : To Taste

Preparation

1 Combine seasoning ingredients in a small bowl.

2 Season mackerel with salt and let sit for 30 minutes. Combine mackerel and half the seasoning with lemon juice and let marinate in refrigerator for at least 1 hour.

3 Place mackerel skin side down on a grill over high heat (or pan, if grill is unavailable). Baste with sauce. Flip after 3~4 minutes and baste again. Continue grilling until fully cooked.

4 Serve garnished with scallion.

4 인분

675g	반으로 가른 고등어
1/2 개	레몬즙
적당량	소금
2 줄기	길게 채 썬 파

양념

간장 3 큰술, 화이트와인 2 큰술, 설탕 1 큰술,
다진 생강 1 ½ 큰술

준비 과정

1 분량의 양념을 볼에 넣어 한데 섞어둡니다.

2 고등어에 소금을 살짝 뿌려 30분 동안 두었다가 레몬즙을 살짝 뿌린 후 절반의 양념에 고등어를 재둡니다.

3 뜨거운 그릴에 껍질 쪽이 밑으로 가도록 먼저 3~4분 정도 구운 다음 뒤집어서 양념의 일부를 바른 후 안쪽을 구워줍니다. 뒤집어서 반대쪽에 양념을 바르고 다시 구워줍니다.

4 접시에 담고 채 썬 파를 올려 상에 냅니다.

Sea Bass with Black Bean Sauce
블랙빈 소스를 곁들인 농어

4 Servings

2	Sea bass fillets (6~8 oz. each)
1 tsp	Garlic, sliced thin
1 tsp	Ginger, sliced thin
6 leaves	Basil leaves, sliced thin
1 stalk	Scallion, julienned
1	Eggplant
As needed	Salt, olive oil

Sauce

3 Tbsp	Soy sauce
2 Tbsp	Black bean sauce
1 Tbsp	White wine
1 tsp	Sesame oil
TT*	Salt, pepper

*TT : To Taste

Preparation

1 Mix sauce ingredients in a large bowl.

2 Season sea bass with salt and pepper.

3 Combine sea bass and sauce with chopped garlic, ginger, and basil leaves.

4 Place the sea bass on a large sheet of foil and fold to cover. Let marinate in refrigerator for at least 30 minutes.

5 Peel eggplant lengthwise using a peeler. Season with salt and olive oil.

6 Broil unwrapped sea bass in a 375°F oven for about 20 minutes.

7 Heat olive oil in large pan over medium-high heat and sauté eggplant until lightly browned.

8 Spoon sauce over a plate and arrange sea bass over strips of eggplant. Garnish with julienned scallions and sauce.

Tip Cod can be substituted for sea bass.

---

4 인분

250 g 짜리	농어 2쪽
1 작은술	채 썬 마늘
1 작은술	채 썬 생강
6 장	채 썬 바질 잎
1 줄기	채 썬 파
1 개	가지
적당량	소금, 올리브오일

소스

간장 3 큰술, 블랙빈 소스 2 큰술, 화이트와인 1 큰술, 참기름 1 작은술, 소금·후추 적당량

준비 과정

1 분량의 소스를 한데 섞어둡니다.

2 농어를 물기 없이 닦아낸 다음 소금과 후추를 뿌려둡니다.

3 준비된 소스를 농어와 잘 섞은 후 채 썬 마늘, 생강, 바질 잎을 넣습니다.

4 소스와 섞은 농어를 알루미늄 호일에 놓고 호일을 접어 오므린 후, 간이 배도록 적어도 30분 간 냉장고에 넣어둡니다.

5 필러를 사용해 가지를 긴 모양이 나오게 한 후 소금과 올리브오일을 살짝 뿌려 둡니다.

6 냉장고에서 농어를 싼 호일을 꺼내 여민 부분을 열어 그대로 190℃로 예열된 오븐에 넣어 20분간 구워냅니다.

7 올리브오일을 두른 중불 프라이팬에 가지를 지져냅니다.

8 가지를 접시에 담고 그 위에 구워진 농어를 올린 후 채 썬 파로 모양을 내고, 밑에 남은 소스를 끼얹어 상에 냅니다.

Tip 농어를 구하지 못하면 대구나 은대구를 사용해도 됩니다.

Miso Black Cod
미소 소스 은대구 구이

4 Servings

4	Black cod fillets (6 oz. each)
1	Zucchini
1	Squash
TT*	Salt, pepper, lemon juice, olive oil

Sauce

2 Tbsp	Miso
3 Tbsp	Brown sugar
1/2 cup	Mirin
1/4 cup	Sake or white wine
TT*	Salt

*TT : To Taste

Preparation

1 Combine sauce ingredients in a small pot and simmer over low heat for 10 minutes or until sauce thickens. Remove from heat and let cool.

2 Season cod with salt, pepper, and lemon juice.

3 Combine cod and sauce in a large plastic bag. Let marinate in refrigerator overnight.

4 Peel zucchini and squash into long strips with a peeler. Season with salt and olive oil.

5 Broil cod (skin side down) in a 375°F oven for 7~10 minutes until cod turns golden brown. Flip cod over and broil for another 5~6 minutes.

6 Heat olive oil in a large pan over medium-high heat and sauté zuchhini and squash.

7 Arrange zucchini and squash around cod and serve.

4 인분

170 g 짜리	은대구 4 쪽
1 개	초록색 호박
1 개	노란색 호박
적당량	소금, 후추, 레몬즙, 올리브오일

양념

일본 된장 2 큰술, 흑설탕 3 큰술, 맛술 1/2 컵, 청주 또는 화이트와인 1/4 컵, 소금 적당량

준비 과정

1 소스 양념을 냄비에 넣고 잘 섞어 약한 불에 10분 정도 조린 후 불을 끄고 소스를 식힙니다.

2 깨끗이 씻은 은대구는 물기를 잘 닦아 소금, 후추, 레몬을 뿌려둡니다.

3 식힌 소스와 은대구를 볼이나 일회용 지퍼백에 넣고 하루 정도 냉장고에 재둡니다.

4 초록색과 노란색 호박은 필러를 사용해 한 끝에서 다른 끝으로 죽 길게 당겨서 긴 모양이 나오도록 한 다음 소금과 올리브오일을 뿌려둡니다.

5 오븐용 팬에 호일을 깔고 은대구를 올린 후 190℃로 예열된 오븐에 구워줍니다. 먼저 은대구 껍질 쪽을 밑으로 놓고 7~10분간 구운 후 노릇노릇해지면 뒤집어서 5~6분간 더 구워줍니다.

6 올리브오일을 두른 중불 프라이팬에 초록색과 노란색 호박을 살짝 볶습니다.

7 은대구와 호박을 접시에 담아 뜨거울 때 상에 냅니다.

Spicy Belt Fish
매운 갈치조림

4 Servings

1½ lb. -1	Belt fish
1 lb.	Radish
3	Green pepper, chopped
1/2 cup	Water

Seasoning

1/2 cup	Water
3 Tbsp	Soy sauce
1 Tbsp	Red pepper paste
3 Tbsp	Dried red pepper powder
1 Tbsp	Fish sauce
1 Tbsp	Sugar
2 tsp	Sesame oil
1½ Tbsp	Garlic, minced
2 tsp	Ginger, minced
1 Tbsp	Salt
TT*	Pepper

*TT : To Taste

Preparation

1 Combine seasoning ingredients in a large bowl.

2 Cut fish into 4~6 pieces. Rinse and pat dry with paper towel.

3 Cut radish into 1/4 -inch thick slices.

4 Place radish, fish, and seasoning in a large pot and bring to a boil. Reduce heat to medium and simmer for another 15 minutes. Stir occasionally.

5 Reduce heat to low and add green peppers. Cover and simmer for another 10~15 minutes.

6 Arrange belt fish over radish and serve with steamed rice.

Tip Mackerel can be substituted for belt fish.

4 인분

675 g 짜리	갈치 1마리
450 g	무
3 개	다진 풋고추
1/2 컵	물

양념
물 1/2 컵, 간장 3 큰술, 고추장 1 큰술, 고춧가루 3 큰술,
피시소스 1 큰술, 설탕 1 큰술, 참기름 2 작은술,
다진 마늘 1½ 큰술, 다진 생강 2 작은술, 소금 1 큰술,
후추 적당량

준비 과정

1 분량의 양념을 한데 섞어둡니다.

2 갈치는 4~6토막 정도로 잘라 깨끗이 씻어 놓습니다.

3 무는 0.5cm 두께로 썰어 놓습니다.

4 밑이 넓은 냄비에 무를 먼저 깔고 그 위에 갈치를 올린 후 준비된 양념을 부어줍니다. 끓으면 불을 줄여 중불에서 15분 정도 조립니다. 중간중간 양념을 끼얹어 줍니다.

5 불을 약하게 줄인 후 풋고추를 넣고 뚜껑을 닫아 10~15분 정도 더 조립니다.

6 갈치와 무를를 보기 좋게 담아 따뜻한 밥과 함께 상에 냅니다.

Tip 고등어와 꽁치, 삼치를 같은 방법으로 조려도 됩니다.

Rather than supplement the meal, Korean soups and stews are often served as the main course. When served with steamed rice and banchan, Korean soups and stews, many times made with beef, pork, chicken, or fish), can make a satisfying meal.

국과 찌개는 주요리로 사용할 정도로 인기 있는 한국음식의 하나입니다. 쇠고기, 돼지고기, 닭고기, 생선이 들어간 국이나 찌개를 밥과 몇 가지 반찬을 곁들여 함께 상에 내면 한 끼 식사로 훌륭하답니다.

Soups & Stews

국과 찌개

Beef Short Rib Soup Galbi Tang 갈비탕

Ginseng Chicken Soup Samghe Tang 삼계탕

Rice Cake Soup 조랭이 떡국

Rice Cake Dumpling Soup Duk Mandu Gook 떡 만두국

Spicy Beef and Vegetable Soup Yookgaejang 육개장

Beef and Noodle Soup 쇠고기 당면국

Bean Sprout · Kimchi · Seaweed Soup 콩나물국, 김치국, 미역국

Soybean Tofu Stew Dwenjang Jigae 된장찌개

Kimchi Stew Kimchi Jigae 김치찌개

Spicy Soft Tofu Stew Soondubu Jigae 순두부찌개

Spicy Pork Belly and Tofu Stew 돼지고기 두부 고추장찌개

Spicy Fish Roe Stew Al Jigae 알찌개

Spicy Cod Stew Daegu Maewoontang 대구 매운탕

Army Stew Budae Jigae 부대찌개

Beef and Vegetable Hot Pot 샤브샤브

Mushroom Hot Pot 버섯전골

Beef Short Rib Soup Galbi Tang
갈비탕

4~6 Servings

2 lb.	Beef short ribs
15 cups	Water
5 cloves	Garlic, peeled
1 oz.	Ginger, peeled
1	Yellow onion
1 lb.	Korean radish
1	Large green onion, sliced thick
2	Eggs, cooked into omelet and sliced thin
1	Scallion, cut diagonally
2 Tbsp	Soy sauce
TT*	Salt, pepper

*TT : To Taste

Preparation

1 Soak beef ribs in cold water for 30 minutes and rinse. Place short ribs in a large pot and bring to a boil with enough water to cover. Remove and rinse short ribs. Rinse the pot.

2 Return short ribs to the pot and add 15 cups of water, garlic, ginger, onion, and radish and boil for 30 minutes over high heat.

3 Discard garlic, ginger, and onion. Remove the radish and cut into thin $1\frac{1}{2}$ -inch squares.

4 Return radish to the pot and add soy sauce, salt, and pepper to taste. Reduce heat to low-medium and simmer for 40 minutes or until short ribs become fork tender. Add large green onion and simmer for another 10 minutes.

5 Serve short rib soup garnished with omelet and scallion.

4~6 인분

900 g	소갈비
15 컵	물
5 쪽	마늘
30 g	생강
1 개	양파
450 g	무
1 줄기분	굵게 썬 대파
2 개분	달걀지단
1 줄기분	어슷 썬 파
2 큰술	간장
적당량	소금, 후추

준비 과정

1 소갈비를 30분 정도 찬물에 담가 핏물을 뺀 다음, 다시 갈비가 덮일 만큼 물을 붓고 끓입니다. 한소끔 끓으면 갈비를 건져내어 깨끗이 씻고 국물을 버린 후 냄비도 깨끗이 한 번 씻습니다.

2 깨끗한 냄비에 갈비를 다시 넣고 물 15컵에 마늘, 생강, 양파, 무를 넣은 후 센 불에서 30분 정도 끓입니다.

3 마늘, 생강, 양파는 건져서 버리고, 무는 꺼내서 가로, 세로 3cm 크기로 납작하게 썬 후 끓고 있는 갈비탕 냄비에 다시 넣습니다.

4 간장, 소금, 후추로 간을 맞춘 후 중불에 갈비가 물렁물렁해질 때까지 40분 정도 더 끓입니다. 대파를 넣고 10분 정도 더 끓인 후 불을 끕니다.

5 국그릇에 갈비와 무를 담고 국물을 부은 후 달걀지단과 어슷 썬 파로 장식하여 상에 냅니다.

Ginseng Chicken Soup Samghe Tang
삼계탕

2~4 Servings

2	Cornish game hens
1 cup	Sweet rice
2 roots	Ginseng
8 cloves	Garlic, peeled
6	Dried dates
10 cups	Water
1 stalk	Scallion, cut diagonally
TT*	Salt, pepper

*TT : To Taste

Preparation

1 Rinse sweet rice and soak in water for 3 hours. Rinse hens, ginseng, garlic, and dried dates. Pat dry with paper towel.

2 Stuff hens with sweet rice, ginseng, garlic, and dates and tie legs together with butcher string.

3 Bring stuffed hens and 10 cups of water to a boil in a large pot. Cook for 20 minutes. Reduce heat to low-medium and simmer for another 30 minutes.

4 Serve either half or whole hen in a large bowl garnished with scallion.

Tip Chicken may be eaten separately dipped in salt and pepper.

2~4 인분

2 마리	작은 닭 (영계)
1 컵	찹쌀
2 뿌리	인삼
8 쪽	마늘
6 개	말린 대추
10 컵	물
1 줄기분	어슷 썬 파
적당량	소금, 후추

준비 과정

1 찹쌀은 깨끗이 씻어 3시간 정도 물에 불려놓고 닭, 인삼, 마늘, 대추도 깨끗이 씻어 준비합니다.

2 닭 뱃속에 찹쌀, 인삼, 마늘과 대추를 넣고 끈으로 두 다리를 묶어줍니다.

3 닭 두 마리를 냄비 속에 안치고 물 10컵을 부어 20분 정도 끓인 후 중불에서 30분 더 끓입니다.

4 커다란 국그릇에 닭 반 마리나 한 마리를 넣고 파를 올려 상에 냅니다.

Tip 닭살은 소금과 후춧가루를 섞어서 찍어 드시면 됩니다.

Ginseng 인삼

Dried dates 대추

Rice Cake Soup
조랭이 떡국

4 Servings

1 lb.	Beef brisket
1	Yellow onion
3 cloves	Garlic, peeled
2 lb.	Jorangyi rice cake
2 stalks	Scallions, cut diagonally
1	Egg, cooked into omelet and cut diagonally

Seasoning

1 Tbsp	Soy sauce
1 Tbsp	Scallion, chopped
1 tsp	Garlic, minced
2 Tbsp	Sesame oil
TT*	Salt, pepper

*TT : To Taste

Preparation

1 Soak brisket in water for 30 minutes. Remove and rinse.

2 Bring brisket, 12 cups of water, onion, and garlic to a boil in a large pot. Reduce heat to low and simmer for 1 hour. Skim surface residue.

3 Discard onions and remove brisket. Tear brisket into bite-sized pieces and marinate with seasoning ingredients.

4 Bring stock back to a boil and add minced garlic, Jorangyi rice cakes, soy sauce, and salt. Add scallions when rice cakes begin to float and cook for a few more minutes.

5 Serve rice cake soup garnished with omelet slices and scallion.

4 인분

450 g	양지머리
1개	양파
3쪽	마늘
900 g	조랭이 떡
2 줄기분	어슷 썬 파
1 개분	달걀지단

고기 양념
국간장 1 큰술, 다진 파 1 큰술, 다진 마늘 1 작은술,
참기름 2 큰술, 소금 · 후추 적당량

준비 과정

1 쇠고기 양지머리를 물에 30분 정도 담가 핏물을 뺍니다.

2 큰 냄비에 양지머리, 양파와 마늘을 넣고 물 12컵을 부어 1시간 정도 삶아냅니다. 물이 끓으면 불을 약하게 줄이고 가장자리에 뜨는 찌거기는 걷어냅니다.

3 양파는 버리고 고기는 건져서 먹기 좋게 찢어 고기 양념에 무쳐 놓습니다.

4 육수를 한소끔 끓이다가 다진 마늘, 조랭이 떡, 국간장과 소금을 넣습니다. 떡이 떠오르면 어슷 썬 파를 넣고 몇 분 더 끓이다 불을 끕니다.

5 그릇에 양념에 무친 고기와 조랭이 떡국을 담고 달걀지단과 어슷 썬 파를 올려 상에 냅니다.

Rice Cake Dumpling Soup

Duk Mandu Gook 떡 만두국

4 Servings

1 lb.	Beef brisket
5 cloves	Garlic, peeled
1 oz.	Ginger, peeled
1	Onion
1 Tbsp	Soy sauce
1 lb.	Rice cake, sliced thin diagonally
2	Eggs, cooked into omelet and sliced thin
2 stalks	Scallion, cut diagonally

Kimchi Dumpling

8 oz.	Pork, ground
18 oz.	Mung bean sprouts
8 oz.	Ripe kimchi
8 oz.	Firm tofu, squeezed
1 pack	Wonton wrappers
2	Eggs, whipped (egg wash)

Seasoning

2 Tbsp	Scallion, chopped
1 Tbsp	Garlic, minced
3 Tbsp	Sesame seeds
2 Tbsp	Sesame oil
2 tsp	Salt
1 tsp	Pepper
TT*	Salt, pepper

*TT : To Taste

Preparation

1 Soak beef brisket in water for 30 minutes and rinse. Bring brisket, 10 cups of water, garlic, ginger, and onion to a boil in a large pot for 45 minutes. Discard garlic, ginger, and onion. Remove brisket and cut into bite-sized pieces. Set aside brisket and stock.

2 Soak rice cakes in water for about 30 minutes. Remove and set aside.

3 Blanch mungbean sprouts and squeeze out excess water. Rinse kimchi and squeeze out excess water. Cut sprouts and kimchi into bite-sized pieces.

4 To make dumpling filling, combine sprouts and kimchi with ground pork, tofu, and seasoning ingredients.

5 Brush ends of a dumpling wrapper with egg wash. Place a small amount of pork and tofu mixture in the middle of the wrapper. Fold the wrapper over the mixture and seal edges.

6 Bring stock back to a boil and add dumplings, brisket, 1 tablespoon of soy sauce, salt, and pepper. Add rice cakes when dumplings begin to float and boil for another 10~15 minutes.

7 Serve garnished with omelet slices and scallion.

4 인분

450 g	양지머리 쇠고기
5 쪽	마늘
30 g	생강
1 개	양파
1 큰술	간장
450 g	떡국 떡
2 개분	달걀지단
2 줄기분	어슷 썬 파

김치만두

갈은 돼지고기 225 g, 숙주 500 g, 김치 225 g, 단단한 두부 225 g, 만두피 1 팩, 어슷 썬 파 2 줄기분, 달걀물 2 개분

양념

다진 파 2 큰술, 다진 마늘 1 큰술, 참깨 3 큰술, 참기름 2 큰술, 소금 2 작은술, 소금 · 후추 적당량

준비 과정

1 양지머리 고기를 30분 정도 찬물에 담가 핏물을 뺀 다음 물 10컵과 마늘, 생강, 양파를 넣고 45분 정도 끓입니다. 마늘, 생강, 양파는 건져내고, 고기는 먹기 좋은 크기로 썰어둡니다.

2 떡은 찬물에 30분 정도 담갔다 꺼내 물기를 빼둡니다.

3 숙주는 뜨거운 물에 데친 후 물기를 꼭 짜고, 김치도 속 부분을 물에 씻어내고 꼭 짠 후 숙주와 김치를 먹기 좋은 크기로 자릅니다.

4 숙주와 김치에 갈은 돼지고기, 물기를 꼭 짠 두부와 분량의 양념을 넣고 잘 섞어 만두 소를 만듭니다.

5 만두피 가장자리에 달걀물을 바르고 소를 한 수저씩 넣고 여며 만두를 만듭니다.

6 준비된 국물이 끓으면 고기와 만두를 넣고 간장 1큰술과 소금, 후추로 간을 합니다. 만두가 떠오르면 떡을 넣고 10~15분 정도 더 끓인 다음 불을 끕니다.

7 그릇에 담고 달걀지단과 파로 장식해 상에 냅니다.

Spicy Beef and Vegetable Soup
Yookgaejang 육개장

4 Servings

1 lb.	Beef brisket
10 cups	Water
5 cloves	Garlic, peeled
1 oz.	Ginger, peeled
2	Large green onion
4 stalks	Scallion
1/2	Yellow onion, sliced
10 oz.	Mung bean sprouts
1	Egg, whisked

Seasoning

2 Tbsp	Dried red pepper powder
1 Tbsp	Red pepper paste
2 Tbsp	Soy sauce
2 Tbsp	Fish sauce
2 Tbsp	Garlic, minced
2 Tbsp	Scallion, chopped
TT*	Salt, pepper

*TT : To Taste

Preparation

1 Combine seasoning ingredients in a small bowl. Set aside.

2 Soak beef brisket in cold water for 30 minutes. Remove and rinse.

3 Bring brisket, 10 cups of water, garlic, and ginger to a boil in a large pot. Reduce heat and simmer for 45 minutes. Skim residue off surface and discard garlic and ginger. Remove brisket, let cool, and shred into bite-sized pieces. Set stock aside.

4 Cut large green onion bulbs in half and soak in water for a few minutes. Cut large green onion and scallion into 2-inch long pieces.

5 Combine brisket, large green onion, scallion, and 2/3 of the seasoning and let marinate for at least 10 minutes.

6 Bring stock back to a boil and add brisket, large green onion, scallion, onions, mung bean sprouts, and the remaining seasoning. Simmer for an additional 30 minutes.

7 Add whisked egg and turn off heat. Serve with steamed rice.

Tip Leeks can be substituted for large green onion.

4 인분

450 g	양지머리 쇠고기
10 컵	물
5 쪽	마늘
30 g	생강
2 줄기	대파
4 줄기	파
1/2 개	채 썬 양파
280 g	숙주
1 개	달걀

양념

고춧가루 2 큰술, 고추장 1 큰술, 간장 2 큰술,
피시소스 2 큰술, 다진 마늘 2 큰술, 다진 파 2 큰술,
소금 · 후추 적당량

준비 과정

1 양념을 한데 섞어둡니다.

2 양지머리 고기를 30분 정도 찬물에 담가 핏물을 뺍니다.

3 큰 냄비에 물 10컵을 붓고 고기, 마늘, 생강을 넣은 후 45분 정도 끓입니다. 끓이면서 중간중간 위에 뜨는 기름과 찌꺼기를 걷어냅니다. 45분 후에 마늘과 생강은 건져서 버리고 고기는 꺼내 식혀 먹기 좋은 크기로 찢어둡니다.

4 대파는 하얀 부분 쪽을 반 갈라 물에 잠시 담가 흙이 빠지게 놔둔 다음 꺼내서 5cm 길이로 잘라 놓고, 파도 5cm 길이로 잘라 놓습니다.

5 고기와 대파, 파를 2/3의 양념에 10분 정도 무쳐 둡니다.

6 고기 끓인 국물에 양념된 고기와 대파, 파, 양파, 숙주를 넣은 다음 나머지 양념을 넣고 30분가량 더 끓입니다.

7 푼 달걀을 위에 끼얹고 불을 끈 후 그릇에 담아 뜨거운 밥과 함께 상에 냅니다.

Beef and Noodle Soup

쇠고기 당면국

4 Servings

4 oz.	Sweet potato starch noodles
1 lb.	Beef brisket
10 cups	Water
1 lb.	Korean radish
1	Onion, yellow
10 cloves	Garlic, peeled
2 stalks	Scallion, cut diagonally
2	Eggs, cooked into omelet and sliced thin
TT*	Salt, pepper

Seasoning

1 Tbsp	Soy sauce
1 tsp	Garlic, minced

*TT : To Taste

Preparation

1 Soak sweet potato starch noodles in warm water until soft.

2 Soak beef brisket in water for 30 minutes. Remove and rinse. Bring brisket and enough water to cover to a boil in medium-sized pot. Remove brisket and rinse pot.

3 Place brisket, radish, onion, garlic, and 10 cups of water in a pot and bring to a boil. Reduce heat to low and simmer covered for 45 minutes. Discard radish, onion, and garlic. Remove brisket and cut into bite-sized pieces. Combine brisket with seasoning ingredients and toss.

4 Return brisket to the pot and bring stock to a boil. Add sweet potato starch noodles and cook for a few more minutes.

5 Add salt and pepper to taste and serve garnished with egg omelet slices and scallion.

4 인분

115 g	당면
450 g	양지머리 쇠고기
10 컵	물
450 g	무
1 개	양파
10 쪽	마늘
2 줄기분	어슷 썬 파
2 개분	달걀지단
적당량	소금, 후추

고기 양념
간장 1 큰술, 다진 마늘 1 작은술

준비 과정

1 당면이 불도록 따뜻한 물에 담가 놓습니다.

2 양지머리는 30분 정도 물에 담가 핏물을 뺀 후 냄비에 고기가 덮일 만큼 물을 붓고 끓입니다. 한소끔 끓으면 고기는 건져내고 냄비는 깨끗이 씻어줍니다.

3 냄비에 건져낸 고기, 무, 양파, 마늘, 물 10컵을 넣고 뚜껑을 닫아 45분 정도 끓인 후 무, 양파, 마늘은 건져버리고 고기는 먹기 좋게 썰어서 양념에 무쳐둡니다.

4 양념에 무친 고기를 다시 고기 국물에 넣고 끓이다가 당면과 파를 넣고 한소끔 끓여줍니다.

5 소금과 후추로 간을 맞춘 후 국그릇에 담고 달걀지단과 파로 장식해 상에 냅니다.

Bean Sprout · Kimchi · Seaweed Soup

콩나물국, 김치국, 미역국

Bean Sprout Soup 콩나물국

4 Servings	
6 cups	Dried anchovy stock (p. 235)
2 cups	Water
10 oz.	Bean sprouts
1 tsp	Garlic, minced
1½ Tbsp	Fish sauce
1	Red pepper, cut diagonally
1 stalk	Scallion, cut diagonally
TT*	Salt, pepper, dried red pepper powder

*TT : To Taste

Preparation

1 Add water to dried anchovy stock and bring to a boil in a large pot. Add bean sprouts, cover pot, and continue to boil for 10 minutes. Add minced garlic and fish sauce and boil covered for another 10 minutes.

2 Add red pepper and scallion and turn off heat. Let sit for 2~3 minutes.

3 Add salt and red pepper powder to taste and serve garnished with scallion.

4 인분	
6 컵	멸치 육수 (p.235)
2 컵	물
285 g	콩나물
1 작은술	다진 마늘
1½ 큰술	피시소스
1 개	어슷 썬 홍고추
1 줄기분	어슷 썬 파
적당량	소금, 후추, 고춧가루

준비 과정

1 준비된 멸치 육수에 물을 더 넣고 끓으면 콩나물을 넣고 뚜껑을 닫은 채 10분 정도 끓입니다. 국물이 끓으면 마늘을 넣고 피시소스로 간을 해 10분 더 끓여줍니다.

2 어슷 썬 홍고추와 파를 넣고 불을 끈 다음 2~3분간 놔둡니다.

3 국물 맛을 보아 기호에 따라 소금을 첨가한 후 국그릇에 담고 어슷 썬 파를 올려 상에 냅니다.

Bean sprouts 콩나물

Kimchi Soup 김치국

4 Servings

4 cups	Dried anchovy stock (p. 235)
1 cup	Water
2 cups	Kimchi, chopped
1 Tbsp	Soy sauce
1/2 Tbsp	Fish sauce
1 tsp	Garlic, minced
8 oz.	Tofu, cut into cubes
1 stalk	Scallion, cut diagonally

Preparation

1 Bring dried anchovy stock and water to a boil in a large pot. Add kimchi, soy sauce, fish sauce, and minced garlic and boil for 15 minutes.

2 Add tofu, reduce heat to low, and let simmer for about 20 minutes.

3 Garnish with scallion and serve with steamed rice.

4 인분

4 컵	멸치 육수 (p. 235)
1 컵	물
2 컵	썬 김치
1 큰술	간장
1/2 큰술	피시소스
1 작은술	다진 마늘
225 g	깍둑 썬 두부
1 줄기분	어슷 썬 파

준비 과정

1 멸치 육수와 물을 넣고 끓기 시작하면 썬 김치, 간장, 피시소스, 마늘을 넣고 15분 정도 끓입니다.

2 두부를 넣고 20분 정도 중불에 끓여줍니다.

3 국그릇에 담고 다진 파를 올려 밥과 함께 상에 냅니다.

Seaweed Soup 미역국

4 Servings

2 oz.	Dried seaweed
4 oz.	Beef, julienned 1-inch long
1 Tbsp	Sesame oil
1 Tbsp	Garlic, minced
2 Tbsp	Soy sauce
2 Tbsp	Fish sauce
12 cups	Water
TT*	Salt

*TT : To Taste

Preparation

1 Soak dried seaweed for about 1 hour in water. Remove and squeeze out excess water. Cut seaweed into 1-inch long slices.

2 Heat sesame oil in a large pot over medium heat and briefly sauté julienned beef and minced garlic. Add seaweed, soy sauce, and fish sauce and sauté for a few more minutes

3 Add 12 cups of water and bring to a boil. Reduce heat to low and simmer for at least 1 hour.

4 Season with salt and serve with steamed rice.

4 인분

55 g	마른 미역
115 g	2.5cm로 채 썬 쇠고기
1 큰술	참기름
1 큰술	다진 마늘
2 큰술	간장
2 큰술	피시소스
12 컵	물
적당량	소금

준비 과정

1 미역은 물에 한 시간 정도 담가 불린 후 물을 꼭 짜 2.5cm 정도의 길이로 잘라 둡니다.

2 큰 냄비에 참기름을 넣고 채 썬 쇠고기와 다진 마늘을 넣고 볶다가 미역, 간장, 피시소스를 넣고 볶습니다.

3 물 12컵을 붓고 끓기 시작하면 불을 줄여 한 시간 정도 끓입니다.

4 싱거우면 소금으로 간을 더하고 국그릇에 담아 밥과 함께 상에 냅니다.

Seaweed 미역

Soybean Tofu Stew
Dwenjang Jigae 된장찌개

4 Servings

1 Tbsp	Butter
2 tsp	Garlic, minced
4 oz.	Lean beef, sliced
1/2	Onion, sliced
6 Tbsp	Soybean paste
4 cups	Dried anchovy stock (p.235)
16 oz.	Tofu, cut into cubes
1	Zucchini, cut into cubes
2	Red peppers, cut diagonally
2	Green peppers, cut diagonally
2 stalks	Scallion, cut diagonally

Preparation

1 Heat butter in a large pot over medium heat. Add minced garlic and beef and sauté until beef just turns color. Add onion and soybean paste and mix thoroughly.

2 Add 4 cups of dried anchovy stock and bring to a boil. Add tofu and zucchini and boil covered for another 5 minutes. Add red and green peppers and boil covered for an additional 5 minutes.

3 Serve garnished with scallion.

4 인분

1 큰술	버터
2 작은술	다진 마늘
110 g	썬 쇠고기
1/2 개분	썬 양파
6 큰술	된장
4 컵	멸치육수(p.235)
450 g	깍둑 썬 두부
1 개분	깍둑 썬 호박
2 개분	어슷 썬 홍고추
2 개분	어슷 썬 풋고추
2 줄기분	어슷 썬 파

준비 과정

1 버터를 두른 냄비에 다진 마늘과 고기를 넣고 볶다가 고기가 다 익으면 양파와 된장을 넣고 타지 않게 잠시 볶다 국물을 붓고 끓입니다.

2 국물이 끓으면 두부와 호박을 넣고 뚜껑을 닫아 5분 정도 더 끓입니다. 다진 홍고추와 고추를 넣고 5분 더 끓인 후 불을 끕니다.

3 어슷 썬 파를 넣고 그릇에 담아 상에 냅니다.

Tip 버터를 쓰면 된장냄새를 줄여주고 고소한 맛을 더 내어 외국인들이 쉽게 접할 수 있습니다.

Kimchi Stew Kimchi Jigae

김치찌개

4 Servings

2 Tbsp	Butter
1 tsp	Garlic, minced
1/2	Onion, julienned
1 lb.	Pork belly, cut into bite-sized pieces
2 lb.	Ripe kimchi, cut into bite-sized pieces
1 pack	Tofu, cut into cubes
1/2 Tbsp	Sugar
1/2 cup	Kimchi juice
1/2 cup	Water
1 stalk	Scallion, cut diagonally

Preparation

1 Melt butter in a large pot over medium-high heat. Add minced garlic and onion and sauté until soft. Add pork belly and then kimchi when pork belly just turns color.

2 Add sugar, kimchi juice, and water and bring to a light boil. Cook for about 30 minutes or until kimchi is tender.

3 Add tofu and continue cooking for another 10 minutes.

4 Garnish with scallion and serve with steamed rice.

4 인분

2 큰술	버터
1 작은술	다진 마늘
1/2 개분	채 썬 양파
450 g	먹기 좋게 썬 돼지고기 삼겹살
900 g	먹기 좋게 썬 익은 김치
1 팩	깍둑 썬 두부
1/2 큰술	설탕
1/2 컵	김치국물
1/2 컵	물
1 줄기분	어슷 썬 파

준비 과정

1 달구어진 팬에 버터를 녹이고 마늘과 양파를 볶다 돼지고기를 넣고 고기가 반쯤 익었을 때 김치를 넣고 같이 볶아줍니다.

2 분량의 설탕과 김치국물, 물을 붓고 끓으면 불을 줄여 김치가 푹 익을 때까지 30분 정도 끓입니다.

3 두부를 넣고 10분 정도 더 끓인 후 불을 끕니다.

4 어슷 썬 파를 넣고 그릇에 김치찌개를 담아 뜨거운 밥과 함께 상에 냅니다.

Spicy Soft Tofu Stew Soondubu Jigae
순두부찌개

4 Servings

4 oz.	Pork belly, sliced thin
4 oz.	Medium-sized shrimp
2 oz.	Mussels
2 oz.	Oysters
8	Little neck clams
22 oz.	Soft tofu
6	Shitake mushrooms
2 stalks	Scallion, cut diagonally
As needed	Grapeseed oil or olive oil
1/3 cup	Water

Seasoning

1 Tbsp	Dried red pepper powder
1 Tbsp	Soy sauce
1 Tbsp	Fish sauce
2 Tbsp	Scallion, chopped
1 tsp	Garlic, minced
1 tsp	Sesame seeds
1 tsp	Sesame oil
TT*	Salt, pepper, dried red peper powder

*TT : To Taste

Preparation

1 Combine seasoning ingredients in a small bowl.

2 Heat grapeseed oil in a large pot over medium-high heat. Add sliced pork and half the seasoning and cook for 2~3 minutes. Add shrimp, mussels, oysters, and clams and cook for another minute.

3 Add soft tofu, water, shitake mushrooms, and remaining seasoning and boil for 10 minutes.

4 Add salt, pepper, and dried red pepper powder as needed. Garnish with scallion and serve with steamed rice.

4 인분

115 g	가늘게 썬 돼지고기 삼겹살
115 g	중간 크기 새우
60 g	홍합
60 g	굴
8 개	바지락 조개
625 g	순두부
6 개	표고버섯
2 줄기분	어슷 썬 파
적당량	포도씨 오일이나 올리브오일
1/3 컵	물

양념

고춧가루 1 큰술, 간장 1 큰술, 피시소스 1 큰술, 다진 파 2 큰술, 다진 마늘 1 작은술, 참깨 1 작은술, 참기름 1 작은술, 소금 · 후추 · 고춧가루 적당량

준비 과정

1 순두부찌개 양념을 한데 섞어둡니다.

2 포도씨 오일을 두른 냄비에 돼지고기와 분량의 양념 절반을 넣고 2~3분 정도 볶다가 새우, 홍합, 굴, 조개를 넣고 같이 볶습니다.

3 순두부를 넣고 물을 부은 후, 표고버섯과 나머지 양념을 넣어 10분 정도 끓입니다.

4 입맛에 따라 소금, 후추, 고춧가루를 더 넣고 그릇에 담은 후, 파를 위에 뿌려 장식을 하고 뜨거운 밥과 함께 상에 냅니다.

Spicy Pork Belly and Tofu Stew
돼지고기 두부 고추장 찌개

4 Servings

1 lb.	Pork belly, cut into 1/2-inch pieces
1	Yellow onion, chopped
1 pack	Tofu, cut into small cubes
1/2 stalk	Large green onion, cut diagonally
2 stalks	Scallions, cut diagonally
5 cups	Water

Seasoning

4 Tbsp	Red pepper paste
1 Tbsp	Dried red pepper powder
2 Tbsp	Soy sauce
1 Tbsp	Salt
2 Tbsp	Scallion, chopped
1 Tbsp	Garlic, minced
1 tsp	Ginger, minced
1 tsp	Sugar
TT*	Pepper

*TT : To Taste

Preparation

1 Combine seasoning ingredients in a smal bowl.

2 Marinate pork belly in half the seasoning for at least 1 hour.

3 Lightly brown pork belly in a large pot. Add onion when pork belly just turns color.

4 Add water and remaining seasoning and boil over medium heat for 30 minutes.

5 Add tofu, large green onion, and scallion and boil for another 15 minutes. Season with salt to taste.

6 Garnish with scallion and serve with steamed rice.

4 인분

450 g	1cm로 썬 돼지고기 삼겹살
1 개분	썬 양파
1 팩	깍둑 썬 두부
1/2 개분	어슷 썬 대파
2 줄기분	어슷 썬 파
5 컵	물

양념

고추장 4 큰술, 고춧가루 1 큰술, 간장 2 큰술, 소금 1 큰술,
다진 파 2 큰술, 다진 마늘 1 큰술, 다진 생강 1 작은술,
설탕 1 작은술, 후추 적당량

준비 과정

1 양념을 한데 섞어둡니다.

2 돼지고기를 분량의 양념 절반과 섞어 한 시간 정도 재둡니다.

3 큰 냄비에 돼지고기를 볶다가 돼지고기가 반 정도 익으면 양파를 넣고 같이 볶아줍니다.

4 물 5컵과 나머지 양념을 넣은 후 한 번 끓으면 중불로 줄여 30분 정도 더 끓입니다.

5 두부와 대파, 파를 넣고 다시 15분 정도 끓인 후 싱거우면 소금으로 간을 더 합니다.

6 국그릇에 담고 어슷 썬 파를 올려 뜨거운 밥과 함께 상에 냅니다.

Spicy Fish Roe Stew Al Jigae
알찌개

4 Servings

1 lb.	Frozen pollack fish roe
5 cups	Dried anchovy stock (p.235)
1	Tofu, cut into small cubes
1/2	Yellow onion, sliced
2 stalks	Scallion, cut diagonally
1	Green pepper, cut diagonally
1	Red pepper, cut diagonally
1 pack	Crown daisies (optional)

Seasoning

2 Tbsp	Dried red pepper powder
2 Tbsp	Fish sauce
1 Tbsp	Soy sauce
1 Tbsp	Garlic, minced
1/2 tsp	Ginger, minced
TT*	Salt, pepper

*TT : To Taste

Preparation

1 Sprinkle salt on frozen fish roe and let sit at room temperature for 2~3 hours. Cut in half lengthwise.

2 Bring dried anchovy stock to a boil in a large pot. Add fish roe, tofu, sliced onions, and chopped green and red peppers. Add seasoning ingredients and continue boiling for 15~20 minutes.

3 Serve garnished with scallion and crown daisies.

4 인분

5 컵	멸치 육수(p.235)
450 g	동태알
1 개분	깍둑 썬 두부
1/2 개분	썬 양파
2 줄기분	어슷 썬 파
1 개	어슷 썬 풋고추
1 개	어슷 썬 홍고추
1 팩	쑥갓 (선택)

양념

고춧가루 2 큰술, 피시소스 2 큰술, 간장 1 큰술,
다진 마늘 1 큰술, 다진 생강 1/2 작은술,
소금·후추 적당량

준비 과정

1 얼린 동태알은 소금을 뿌린 후 간이 배게 2~3시간 정도 실온에 꺼내 둡니다. 세로로 반을 갈라 사용하기 전까지 냉장고에 둡니다.

2 준비해 둔 멸치 육수를 냄비에 붓고 끓으면 소금간이 밴 동태알을 넣습니다. 다시 한소끔 끓으면 두부, 양파, 풋고추, 홍고추를 넣고 준비된 양념을 같이 넣어 15~20분 정도 더 끓인 후 불을 끕니다.

3 그릇에 담고 파와 쑥갓을 올려 상에 냅니다.

Tip 알 하나 정도는 터뜨리고 알을 충분히 넣어야 국물 맛이 훨씬 좋습니다.

Spicy Cod Stew Daegu Maewoontang
대구 매운탕

4 Servings

6 cups	Water
1lb.	Radish, cut into thin 1 $\frac{1}{2}$ -inch squares
1	Medium onion, sliced thick
2 $\frac{1}{2}$ lb.	Cod, cut into 3-inch long pieces
12 oz.	Zucchini, cut into 1/4-inch thick pieces
1 pack	Tofu, cut into 1 $\frac{1}{2}$ -inch squares
2	Red peppers, cut diagonally
1 pack	Crown daisies

Soup Seasoning

2 Tbsp	Red pepper paste
1 Tbsp	Dried red pepper powder
2 Tbsp	Fish sauce
1 Tbsp	Soy sauce
1 tsp	Salt
2 tsp	Garlic, minced
1/2 tsp	Ginger, minced
1 stalk	Scallion, chopped

Preparation

1 Combine seasoning in a medium-sized bowl.

2 Bring 6 cups of water and seasoning ingredients to a boil. Add radish when stock reaches a boil. Add onions when radish is cooked halfway through.

3 Add cod, zucchini, tofu, and red pepper and boil for 15 minutes.

4 Add crown daisies and remove pot from heat. Serve with steamed rice.

Tip Dried anchovy stock can be substituted for water.

4 인분

6컵	물
450 g	가로 세로 3cm로 얇게 썬 무
1 개분	두껍게 채 썬 중간 크기 양파
1 kg	토막 낸 대구
340 g	0.5cm로 썬 호박
1 팩	가로 세로 3cm로 썬 두부
2 개분	어슷 썬 홍고추
1 팩	쑥갓

국물 양념

고추장 2 큰술, 고춧가루 1 큰술, 피시소스 2 큰술, 간장 1 큰술, 소금 1 작은술, 다진 마늘 2 작은술, 다진 생강 1/2 작은술, 다진 파 1 줄기분

준비 과정

1 국물 양념 재료를 미리 섞어둡니다.

2 물 6컵과 양념을 함께 끓입니다. 물이 끓으면 무를 먼저 넣고 20분 정도 끓여 무가 반쯤 익으면 양파를 넣습니다.

3 한소끔 끓으면 대구, 호박, 두부, 홍고추를 넣고 끓입니다.

4 15분 정도 끓인 후 쑥갓을 넣고 불을 끈 후 볼에 담아 따뜻한 밥과 함께 상에 냅니다.

Tip 물 대신 멸치 육수를 사용하면 맛이 더욱 좋습니다.

Army Stew Budae Jigae
부대찌개

4 Servings

As needed	Olive oil
1/2 cup	Ripe kimchi, cut into bite-sized pieces
2 cups	Chicken broth
2 cups	Water
1	Yellow onion, sliced
12 oz. can	Spam, cut into 1/4 x 2-inch squares
4	Hot dogs, cut diagonally
1	Zucchini, cut into half moons
1/4	Cabbage, cut into 2-inch squares
15 oz.	Pork and beans, drained
2 stalks	Scallion, cut diagonally
2 packs	Ramen, noodles only
1~2 slices	American cheese (optional)
TT*	Pepper

Seasoning

1 Tbsp	Red pepper paste
1 1/2 tsp	Dried red pepper powder
1/2 tsp	Garlic, minced
TT*	Salt, pepper

*TT : To Taste

Preparation

1 Heat olive oil in a large pot over medium heat. Add kimchi and sauté until lightly browned. Add chicken stock and water and bring to a boil over medium-high heat until kimchi is tender.

2 Add onions and boil for another 3~4 minutes. Add spam, hot dogs, and zucchini and simmer over low-medium heat for 10 minutes. Add cabbage, pork and beans, scallion, and seasoning and let simmer for 5~7 minutes. Add salt to taste.

3 Meanwhile bring a small pot of water to a boil and cook noodles for 2 minutes.

4 Add noodles to the stew and let simmer for another 1~2 minutes.

5 Place a slice of American cheese in each bowl (optional) and serve with steamed rice.

4 인분

적당량	올리브오일
1/2 컵	먹기 좋게 썬 익은 김치
2 컵	닭고기 육수
2 컵	물
1 개분	썬 양파
340 g 짜리 캔	1cm 두께, 5cm 길이로 썬 스팸
4 개분	어슷 썬 프랑크 소시지
1 개분	반달 모양으로 썬 호박
1/4 개분	가로 세로 5cm 로 썬 양배추
425 g 짜리 캔	통조림 콩
2 줄기분	어슷 썬 파
2 봉지	라면 (면만)
1~2 장	슬라이스 치즈 (선택)
적당량	후추

양념
고추장 1 큰술, 고춧가루 1½ 작은술, 다진 마늘 1/2 작은술,
소금 · 후추 적당량

준비 과정

1 냄비나 전골 냄비에 올리브오일 1큰술 정도를두르고 썬 김치를 타지 않게 볶다가 분량의 닭고기 육수와 물을 붓고 끓입니다.

2 김치가 좀 익도록 한소끔 끓이다 양파를 넣고 3~4분 정도 더 끓입니다. 스팸, 소시지, 호박을 넣고 10분 정도 중불에 끓여줍니다. 양배추와 체에 건진 통조림 콩, 파와 양념을 넣은 후 스팸과 소시지에서 맛이 우러나도록 약한 불에서 좀 더 끓여줍니다. 간을 보고 싱거우면 소금을 조금 더 넣어줍니다.

3 작은 냄비에 물을 끓여 라면 면을 미리 2분 정도 삶아 준비합니다. 그래야 부대찌개 국물이 줄어들지 않습니다.

4 먹기 전에 삶아 둔 라면을 같이 넣고 1~2분 정도 더 끓인 후 불을 끕니다.

5 개인 그릇에 조금씩 떠서 담은 후 치즈를 위에 올려 뜨거운 밥과 함께 드시면 좋습니다.

Beef and Vegetable Hot Pot

샤브샤브

4 Servings

8 ~ 12 cups	Beef stock (p.234)
2 lb.	Beef, sliced thin
4	Bok choy
1	Yellow onion, sliced
4	Napa cabbage leaves
4	King oyster mushrooms
1 pack	Enoki mushrooms
4 stalks	Scallion, cut into 2-inch pieces

Dipping Sauce

4	Egg yolks
4 Tbsp	Pon shabu sauce
2 Tbsp	Goma shabu sauce

Preparation

1 Place 1 tablespoon of pon shabu sauce in a serving bowl. Place 1/2 tablespoon of goma shabu sauce in a serving bowl. Add an egg yolk to each.

2 Bring beef stock to a boil in a hot pot. Reduce heat and add beef and vegetables.

3 Hot pots are communal and self-served.

Tip Other vegetables may be added to the hot pot as desired.

4 인분

8 ~ 12 컵	쇠고기 육수 (p.234)
900 g	차돌박이
4 개	청경채
1 개분	썬 양파
4 장	배춧잎
4 개	새송이버섯
1 팩	팽이버섯
4 줄기분	5cm 길이로 썬 파

찍어 먹는 소스

달걀노른자 4 개분, 간장 샤브 소스 4 큰술, 미소 샤브 소스 2 큰술

준비 과정

1 1인분 용 찍어 먹는 소스를 만들기 위해 간장 샤브 소스 1큰술과 미소 샤브 소스 반 큰술을 소스 그릇에 담고 달걀노른자 하나씩을 올립니다.

2 쇠고기 육수를 전골 냄비에 넣고 끓입니다. 육수가 끓기 시작하면 불을 줄이고 고기, 채소, 버섯을 넣고 살짝 익혀 소스에 찍어 드시면 됩니다.

3 전골은 함께 드시거나 작은 전골 냄비를 사용해 1인분씩 끓여가며 드셔도 됩니다.

Tip 좋아하는 다른 야채를 첨가해도 좋습니다.

Goma Shabu 미소 샤브 소스

Pon Shabu 간장 샤브 소스

Mushroom Hot Pot

버섯전골

4 Servings

1 lb.	Beef rib eye, sliced
4	King oyster mushrooms
4	Shitake mushrooms
1 pack	Oyster mushrooms
1 pack	Enoki mushrooms
1 pack	Bell button mushrooms
1	Yellow onion
1	Carrot
1	Zucchini
1	Tofu
1 cup	Large green onion, cut diagonally
6~8 cups	Beef stock (p.234)

Seasoning

3 Tbsp	Soy sauce
1 Tbsp	Sugar
1 tsp	Garlic, minced
1 tsp	Sesame oil
TT*	Pepper

Dipping Sauce

6 Tbsp	Soy sauce
6 Tbsp	Water
2 tsp	Vinegar
1 tsp	Dijon mustard
4 tsp	Sugar
1/2 tsp	Garlic, minced
1/2 tsp	Ginger, minced
4	Egg yolks (optional)

*TT : To Taste

Preparation

1 Combine dipping sauce ingredients in a small bowl.

2 Combine meat with seasoning ingredients and let marinate for at least 1 hour.

3 Cut mushrooms, onion, carrot, zucchini, and tofu into medium-sized pieces.

4 Layer onions, mushrooms, carrot, zucchini, and tofu around a hot pot. Repeat as necessary. Add beef to the middle and place large green onion on top. Add stock and bring to a boil.

5 Add egg yolk (optional) to each individually served dipping sauce. Hot pots are communal and self-served.

4 인분

450 g	불고기감 쇠고기
4개	새송이 버섯
4개	표고버섯
1팩	느타리버섯
1팩	팽이버섯
1팩	양송이버섯
1개	양파
1개	당근
1개	애호박
1팩	두부
1컵	어슷 썬 대파
6~8 컵	쇠고기 육수 (p. 234)

불고기 양념
간장 3 큰술, 설탕 1 큰술, 다진 마늘 1 작은술,
참기름 1 작은술, 후추 적당량

찍어 먹는 소스
간장 4 큰술, 물 6 큰술, 식초 2 작은술,
머스터드 1 작은술, 설탕 4 작은술, 다진 마늘 1/2 작은술,
다진 생강 1/2 작은술, 후추 적당량, 달걀노른자 4 개 (선택)

준비 과정

1 찍어 먹는 소스 재료를 한데 섞어둡니다.

2 양념을 한데 섞은 후 쇠고기를 넣고 잘 섞어 한 시간 정도 재둡니다.

3 모든 버섯과 양파, 당근, 호박, 두부는 먹기 좋은 크기로 썰어둡니다.

4 큰 전골 냄비에 양파, 버섯, 당근, 애호박, 두부 순으로 돌려 놓고 가운데에 불고기를 올린 다음 대파를 올리고 전골 국물을 부어 끓입니다.

5 기호에 따라 소스에 달걀노른자를 넣고 찍어 드시면 좋습니다.

Tip 육수를 넣을 때 입맛에 맞게 소금간을 조금 하면 맛이 더 살아납니다.

Rice is the primary source of carbs for Koreans. Rice is included in nearly every Korean meal, either steamed or as part of a dish.

한국 사람들은 대부분 빵보다는 밥으로 주식을 하는 경우가 많습니다. 한국 사람들은 거의 모두 끼니마다 밥이나 밥으로 만든 단품 요리를 즐겨 먹습니다.

Rice Dishes

밥

Rice Porridge in Three Acts - Pine Nut, Black Sesame Seed, Butternut Squash 잣죽, 흑임자죽, 단호박죽

Rice with Beef and Vegetables Bibim Bop 비빔밥

Kimchi Risotto in Peppers 김치 리조토

Curry Rice 카레밥

Hot Stone Rice with Squid Ojinguh Dolsot Bop 오징어 돌솥밥

Spicy Rice and Sashimi Hwae Dupbop 회덮밥

Rice and Vegetable Pockets 유부초밥

Sushi 초밥

Kimbop 김밥

Vegetable Wraps with Rice Ssambop 쌈밥정식

Rice Porridge in Three Acts - Pine Nut, Black Sesame Seed, Butternut Squash

잣죽 · 흑임자죽 · 단호박죽

Pine Nut Porridge 잣죽

4 Servings
1 cup	Rice, uncooked
1 cup	Pine nuts
4 cups	Water
TT*	Salt, sugar

*TT : To Taste

Preparation

1 Rinse rice and soak in water for 2~3 hours. Drain water and set rice aside.

2 Place rice, pine nuts, and 4 cups of water in a blender. Blend well and strain to remove husks and skins.

3 Simmer mixture in a medium-sized pot for 15~20 minutes. Stir frequently to prevent bottom from burning.

4 When soup achieves desired thickness, remove from heat and add salt and sugar to taste.

5 Serve warm or chilled.

Tip If preparing in advance, blend rice and pine nuts separately in equal amounts of water.

4 인분
1 컵	쌀
1 컵	잣
4 컵	물
적당량	소금, 설탕

준비 과정

1 쌀은 깨끗이 씻어 2~3시간 동안 물에 불린 다음 체에 밭쳐 놓습니다.

2 쌀과 잣을 믹서에 넣고 물 4컵 정도를 부어 간 후 찌꺼기가 없도록 체에 한 번 걸러줍니다.

3 믹서에 간 재료를 냄비에 넣고 15~20분 정도 약한 불에 끓이면서 밑부분이 눌지 않도록 저어 줍니다.

4 걸쭉한 상태가 되면 불을 끄고 기호에 따라 소금과 설탕을 넣습니다.

5 따뜻하게 드셔도 좋고 차게 드셔도 맛있습니다.

Tip 죽을 두었다 드실 때는 쌀과 잣을 따로따로 갈아서 쓰면 좋습니다.

Black Sesame Seed Porridge 흑임자죽

4 Servings

1 cup	Rice, uncooked
1 cup	Black sesame seeds
6 cups	Water
TT*	Salt, sugar

*TT : To Taste

Preparation

1 Rinse rice and soak in water for 2~3 hours. Drain water and set rice aside.

2 Toast black sesame seeds in a small pan over medium-low heat until fragrant. Remove seeds from heat and let cool.

3 Blend rice and black sesame seeds with 6 cups of water in a blender. Strain well.

4 Bring mixture to a boil in a large pot, stirring occasionally. Reduce heat and simmer for 20~30 minutes. Stir frequently to prevent bottom from burning.

5 Add salt and sugar to taste immediately before serving.

Tip ¹ If preparing in advance, blend rice and black sesame seeds separately in equal amounts of water.

² Add water while soup is boiling if consistency becomes too thick.

4 인분

1 컵	쌀
1 컵	검은깨
6 컵	물
적당량	소금, 설탕

준비 과정

1 쌀은 깨끗이 씻어 2~3 시간 동안 물에 불린 다음 체에 밭쳐 놓습니다.

2 검은깨는 프라이팬에 볶아 식힙니다.

3 쌀과 깨를 믹서에 넣고 물 6 컵 정도를 부어 간 후 체에 한 번 걸러줍니다.

4 큰 냄비에 믹서에 간 재료를 넣고 나무 주걱으로 저어주다가 가운데가 보글보글 끓어오르면 불을 줄여 20~30분 정도 약한 불에 끓이면서 밑 부분이 눌지 않도록 저어줍니다.

5 기호에 따라 먹기 직전 소금이나 설탕을 넣어 드시면 됩니다.

Tip ¹ 죽을 두었다 드실 때는 쌀과 검은깨를 따로따로 갈아서 쓰면 좋습니다.

² 너무 되게 끓여지면 물을 좀 더 넣어야 됩니다.

Butternut Squash Porridge 단호박죽

4 Servings

1/2 cup	Rice, uncooked
As needed	Vegetable oil
1	Large yellow onion, chopped
1 stalk	Celery, chopped
1 stalk	Leek, bulb only, chopped
2 lb.	Butternut squash, peeled and cut into 1/2-inch cubes
4 cups	Chicken stock
1 cup	Water
1	Small apple, cut into 1/2-inch cubes
1 cup	Heavy whipping cream
1 tsp	Salt
TT*	Salt

*TT : To Taste

Preparation

1 Rinse rice and soak in water for 1 hour. Drain water and set rice aside.

2 Heat vegetable oil in a large pot over medium heat. Add onion, celery, and leek and sauté for about 7 minutes or until tender.

3 Add butternut squash, rice, chicken stock, and enough water to cover. Bring to a boil and cook for 25~30 minutes or until squash is tender.

4 Add apple and whipping cream and continue to boil for another three minutes.

5 Add salt and puree ingredients in a blender. Serve immediately.

4 인분

1/2 컵	쌀
적당량	식용유
1 개분	굵게 다진 양파
1 줄기	다진 셀러리
1 줄기	다진 대파 흰 부분만
900 g	깍둑 썬 단호박
4 컵	닭고기 육수
1 컵	물
1 개분	1 cm로 깍둑 썬 작은 사과
1 컵	생크림
1 작은술	소금
적당량	소금

준비 과정

1 쌀은 물에 씻어 1시간 정도 불린 후 체에 받쳐 둡니다.

2 중불 프라이팬에 식용유를 두르고 양파, 셀러리, 파를 넣고 7분 정도 볶아줍니다.

3 양파가 익은 듯하면 단호박과 쌀, 닭고기 육수를 넣고 야채가 다 잠기지 않으면 물을 조금 더 넣어서 호박이 익을 때까지 25~30분 정도 끓입니다.

4 사과와 생크림을 넣고 3분 정도 끓입니다.

5 소금으로 간을 한 후 믹서에 갈아 그릇에 담고 상에 냅니다.

Rice with Beef and Vegetables Bibim Bop
비빔밥

4 Servings

1 lb.	Beef sirloin, sliced
4	Kirby cucumbers, cut diagonally
1	Carrot, julienned
1 pack	Shitake mushrooms, sliced
8 oz.	Bean sprouts
3 cups	Steamed rice
2	Eggs, cooked into omelet and sliced thin
TT*	Minced garlic, salt, pepper, sesame oil, sesame seeds
As needed	Vegetable oil

Seasoning

1 Tbsp	Soy sauce
1 Tbsp	Brown sugar
1 tsp	Garlic, minced
2 tsp	Sesame seeds
1 tsp	Sesame oil
TT*	Pepper

Sauce

3 Tbsp	Red pepper paste
3 Tbsp	Sesame oil

*TT : To Taste

Preparation

1 Rinse 2 cups of rice and steam in rice cooker with $1\frac{3}{4}$ cups of water.

2 Combine seasoning ingredients in a medium-sized bowl. Add beef and let marinate for 20 minutes. Heat vegetable oil in a large pan over medium-high heat and sauté beef until desired doneness. Set aside.

3 Sprinkle salt on cucumber and let sit for at least 30 minutes. Squeeze out excess water.

4 Heat oil in a large pan over medium-high heat. Sauté cucumbers, carrots, and mushrooms each for 5~6 minutes. Add salt and garlic to taste while cooking. Set aside.

5 Boil bean sprouts, 1/2 teaspoon of garlic, and salt in 1 cup of water over high heat. Drain water and toss sprouts in sesame oil and sesame seeds.

6 Arrange 3/4 cup of steamed rice, beef, and vegetables in individual bowls. Garnish with omelet slices and serve with red pepper paste sauce and sesame oil on the side.

4 인분

450 g	채 썬 쇠고기
4 개분	어슷 썬 오이
1 개분	가늘게 채 썬 당근
1 팩	썬 버섯
225 g	콩나물
3 컵	밥
2 개분	달걀지단
적당량	다진 마늘, 소금, 후추, 참기름, 참깨
적당량	식용유

고기 양념

간장 1 큰술, 흑설탕 1 큰술, 다진 마늘 1 작은술,
참깨 2 작은술, 참기름 1 작은술, 후추 적당량

고추장 소스

고추장 3 큰술, 참기름 3 큰술

준비 과정

1 전기밥솥에 깨끗이 씻은 쌀 2 컵과 물 $1\frac{3}{4}$ 컵을 부어 밥을 짓습니다.

2 양념 재료를 한데 섞고 채 썬 쇠고기를 20분 정도 재두었다가 식용유를 두른 뜨거운 팬에 볶아줍니다.

3 오이는 소금을 살짝 뿌려 30분 정도 두었다 물기를 꼭 짜줍니다.

4 뜨거운 팬에 식용유를 두르고 오이와 당근, 버섯을 각각 따로 5~6분 정도 볶아줍니다. 소금과 마늘을 넣어가며 간을 봅니다.

5 콩나물은 냄비에 담고 물 1컵과 다진 마늘 1/2작은술, 소금을 넣어 뚜껑을 닫고 센 불에 5분 정도 끓인 후 꺼내서 참기름과 참깨로 버무려 놓습니다.

6 큰 그릇에 밥 3/4컵을 담고, 볶은 쇠고기, 오이, 당근, 버섯, 콩나물, 달걀지단을 올린 후 고추장 소스와 참기름을 곁들여 상에 냅니다. 식성에 따라 고추장 소스와 참기름의 양을 조절해 드시면 됩니다.

Kimchi Risotto in Peppers
김치 리조토

4 Servings

4	Large bell peppers
1 cup	Rice, uncooked
2 cups	Chicken stock
1 oz.	Butter
1 oz.	Bacon, diced
2 Tbsp	Red wine
1 cup	Onion, chopped
1 cup	Ripe kimchi, sliced thin
1 cup	Shitake mushrooms, sliced
TT *	Mozzarella cheese, shredded
As needed	Vegetable oil

* TT : To Taste

Preparation

1 Rinse rice and soak in water for 30 minutes. Drain water and set rice aside.

2 Simmer chicken stock until warm.

3 Cut tops off bell peppers and core competely. Rinse and set aside.

4 Heat vegetable oil in a large pan over medium-high heat and sauté bacon for 3~4 minutes. Add red wine and reduce by half. Add onion, kimchi, rice, mushrooms, and butter. Sauté for 3~4 minutes.

5 Add chicken stock and simmer in low heat for 15 minutes. Stir occasionally and remove from heat when rice is al dente.

6 Stuff bell peppers with rice mixture and bake in a 400°F oven for 15~20 minutes. Add mozzarella cheese on top and bake until cheese is golden brown.

7 Serve stuffed peppers garnished with parsley.

4인분

4 개	큰 피망
1 컵	쌀
2 컵	닭고기 육수
30 g	버터
30 g	썬 베이컨
2 큰술	레드와인
1 컵	잘게 썬 양파
1 컵	가늘게 썬 익은 김치
1 컵	채 썬 표고버섯
적당량	모차렐라 치즈
적당량	식용유

준비 과정

1 쌀은 깨끗이 씻어 물에 30분가량 불려둡니다.

2 닭고기 육수는 적당히 데워둡니다.

3 피망은 윗 부분을 잘라내고 속을 개끗이 씻어둡니다.

4 뜨거운 팬에 식용유를 두르고 베이컨을 3~4분쯤 볶다가 레드와인을 넣습니다. 와인이 반 정도로 증발되면 양파와 김치, 쌀, 버섯, 버터를 넣고 3~4분 정도 더 볶습니다.

5 닭고기 육수 데운 것을 붓고 약한 불에 15분 정도 끓이면서 쌀이 다 익은 듯할 때 불을 끕니다. 중간중간 밑이 눌어붙지 않게 저어줍니다.

6 피망에 볶아진 재료를 채워서 미리 예열한 200℃ 오븐에 15~20분 정도 굽다 모차렐라 치즈를 뿌리고 노릇해질 때까지 다시 구워줍니다.

7 오븐에서 꺼내 개인 접시나 큰 접시에 담고 파슬리를 뿌려 상에 냅니다.

Curry Rice

카레밥

4 Servings

1 oz.	Butter
1 lb.	Stew beef, cut into cubes
TT*	Salt, pepper
2	Idaho potatoes, cut into cubes
1	Carrot, cut into cubes
1	Onion, cut into cubes
4 Tbsp	Peas, cooked
5 cups	Water
8 oz.	Curry cake, crumbled
4 cups	Steamed rice

*TT : To Taste

Preparation

1 Melt butter in a large pot over medium-high heat. Add beef, salt, and pepper and cook until beef just turns color. Add potatoes, carrot, and onion and cook until onions become translucent.

2 Add 5 cups of water and simmer for 30 minutes over medium heat.

3 Add peas and curry. Simmer for another 5~7 minutes. Stir occasionally.

4 Serve over steamed rice.

4 인분

30 g	버터
450 g	깍둑 썬 스튜용 쇠고기
적당량	소금, 후추
2 개분	깍둑 썬 감자
1 개분	깍둑 썬 당근
1 개분	깍둑 썬 양파
4 큰술	익은 완두콩
5 컵	물
225 g	고형 카레
4 컵	밥

준비 과정

1 냄비에 버터를 넣고 녹으면 먹기 좋게 썬 고기를 넣은 후 소금, 후추와 함께 볶습니다. 고기 색이 갈색으로 변하면 감자, 당근, 양파를 넣고 양파가 익을 때까지 볶아줍니다.

2 물 5컵을 붓고 끓으면 불을 줄여 30분 정도 더 끓입니다.

3 익은 완두콩을 넣고, 고형 카레를 잘게 잘라 넣습니다. 가끔씩 저어주면서 고형 카레가 녹을 때까지 5~7분 정도 더 끓입니다.

4 따뜻한 밥 위에 카레를 올려 상에 냅니다.

Curry cake 고형 카레

Curry powder 카레가루

Hot Stone Rice with Squid

Ojinguh Dolsot Bop 오징어 돌솥밥

4 Servings

3 cups	Rice
3 cups	Water
As needed	Sesame oil
4 cups	Stir-fried spicy squid (p.114)
1 cup	Dried seaweed, sliced
TT*	Sesame oil, sesame seeds

*TT : To Taste

Preparation

1 Rinse rice and drain water. Add water to rice in a medium-sized pot. Bring to a boil, stirring occasionally. Reduce heat to low and let simmer covered for 20 minutes. Turn off heat and let sit for another 10 minutes covered.

2 Lightly brush the bottom of four stone bowls with sesame oil. Evenly spread out one cup of cooked rice inside each bowl.

Add stir-fried spicy squid and place bowls on a range over medium heat for 15~20 minutes (until the rice toasting at the bottom is light brown).

3 Remove from heat with proper utensils or heavy gloves.

4 Garnish with seaweed and sesame seeds. Drizzle lightly with sesame oil and serve immediately.

Tip Cooked shrimp, mussels, and oysters can also be added.

---

4 인분

3 컵	쌀
3 컵	물
적당량	참기름
4 컵	오징어 볶음 (p.114)
1 컵	채 썬 김
적당량	참기름, 참깨

준비 과정

1 쌀을 깨끗이 씻어 물기를 완전히 뺀 후 중간 크기 냄비에 쌀과 분량의 물을 넣고 끓입니다. 밑이 눌지 않도록 수저로 저어줍니다. 끓기 시작하면 불을 약하게 줄이고 뚜껑을 닫아 20분 정도 끓입니다. 불을 끄고 뚜껑을 덮은 채로 10분 정도 둡니다.

2 4개의 돌솥 밑부분에 밥이 붙지 않도록 참기름을 살짝 바르고, 밥 한 컵씩을 넓게 편 다음 오징어 볶음을 올리고, 중간 불에 15~20분 정도 둡니다. 가끔 밥이 타는지 밑부분을 봐줍니다.

3 돌솥에서 지글지글 거리는 소리가 나면서 밥이 연한 갈색으로 변하면 불에서 내립니다. 돌솥이 뜨거우니 손이 데지 않도록 장갑이나 다른 도구를 사용합니다.

4 채 썬 김을 올리고 참깨를 뿌려 상에 냅니다. 식성에 따라 참기름을 조금 더 넣어도 좋습니다.

Tip 새우와 홍합, 굴 등을 이용하여 해물 돌솥밥을 만들 수도 있습니다.

Spicy Rice and Sashimi Hwae Dupbop

회덮밥

4 Servings

4 cups	Steamed rice
1 lb.	Sashimi-grade tuna, cut into 1/4-inch cubes
1/2 lb.	Sashimi-grade salmon, cut into 1/4-inch cubes
1 lb.	Cooked octopus, cut into 1/4-inch pieces
1	Romaine lettuce, cut into bite-sized pieces
4	Kirby cucumber, julienned
1	Carrot, julienned
2 packs	Radish sprouts, roots removed
8	Radish, sliced thin
As needed	Sesame oil

Sauce

4 Tbsp	Red pepper paste
2 Tbsp	White wine vinegar
3 Tbsp	Sprite or other lime soda
1½ Tbsp	Brown sugar
1 Tbsp	Sesame seeds
1 tsp	Garlic, minced

Preparation

1 Combine sauce ingredients in a small bowl. Set aside.

2 Rinse vegetables and drain.

3 Place 1 cup of steamed rice inside 4 medium-sized bowls (1 cup of rice per bowl). Arrange vegetables, sashimi, and octopus over the rice in each bowl.

4 Serve with sauce and sesame oil on the side.

Tip ¹ Any kind of sashimi can be used.

² Various fish roes, such as salted pollack roe, salmon roe, and flying fish roe, can be substituted for sashimi.

4 인분

4 컵	밥
450 g	0.5 cm로 깍둑 썬 참치회
225 g	0.5 cm로 깍둑 썬 연어회
450 g	0.5 cm로 깍둑 썬 익은 문어
1 장	먹기 좋게 썬 로메인 레터스
4 개분	채 썬 오이
1 개분	채 썬 당근
2 팩	무순
8 개분	얇게 저며 썬 래디시
적당량	참기름

초고추장

고추장 4 큰술, 화이트와인 식초 2 큰술, 사이다 3 큰술, 흑설탕 1½ 큰술, 참깨 1 큰술, 다진 마늘 1 작은술

준비 과정

1 소스 재료는 작은 볼에 넣고 한데 섞어둡니다.

2 야채를 썰고 무순은 밑동을 잘라 깨끗이 씻어 준비합니다.

3 갓 지은 밥을 한 컵씩 4개의 그릇에 담고 야채와 생선회, 익은 문어를 올립니다.

4 초고추장과 참기름을 식성에 맞게 넣어 밥과 비벼 먹습니다.

Tip ¹ 다른 생선 종류를 사용해도 됩니다.

² 생선회 대신 연어알이나 날치알, 명태알을 밥 위에 올리고 참기름과 간장을 넣고 비벼 드셔도 좋습니다.

Rice and Vegetable Pockets
유부초밥

4 Servings (20 pieces)

1 pack	Fried bean curd pockets
1/2 lb.	Carrot, julienned 1/2-inch long
1/2 lb.	Burdock, julienned 1/2-inch long
1/2 lb.	Shitake mushrooms, sliced thin
6 cups	Steamed rice
2 Tbsp	Vinegar powder
As needed	Vegetable oil
As needed	Black sesame seeds

Seasoning

1/2 cup	Soy sauce
1/2 cup	Mirin
3 Tbsp	Sugar
3 Tbsp	Water

Preparation

1 Combine seasoning ingredients in a small bowl.

2 Boil fried bean curd pockets in a medium-sized pot for 3 to 4 minutes. Remove and cut pockets in half. Gently squeeze out excess water.

3 Heat vegetable oil in a large pan over medium heat. Add pockets and sauté with 3~4 tablespoons of seasoning until lightly browned. Remove and set aside.

4 Add oil to the same pan and sauté carrots, burdock, and mushrooms with 10 tablespoons of seasoning for 7~10 minutes.

5 Combine steamed rice with 2 tablespoons of vinegar powder, sautéed carrots, burdock, and mushrooms in a large bowl.

6 Stuff pockets with rice mixture, garnish with black sesame seeds, and serve.

Tip Most Asian markets carry cooked bean curd pockets.

4 인분 (20개)

1 팩 (20개)	유부
225 g	1 cm로 채 썬 당근
225 g	1 cm로 채 썬 우엉
225 g	가늘게 썬 표고버섯
6 컵	밥
2 큰술	식초가루
적당량	식용유
적당량	검은깨

양념
간장 1/2 컵, 맛술 1/2 컵, 설탕 3 큰술, 물 3 큰술

준비 과정

1 양념을 작은 볼에 넣어 한데 섞어둡니다.

2 끓는 물에 네모난 유부를 넣고 3~4분간 데쳐 꺼내서 반으로 잘라 물기를 살짝 짭니다.

3 중불 프라이팬에 식용유를 두르고, 유부를 볶다가 양념 3~4큰술을 넣고 볶아둡니다.

4 프라이팬에 식용유를 더 두르고, 당근, 우엉, 버섯에 양념 10큰술을 섞어 7~10분 정도 볶아 놓습니다.

5 큰 그릇에 밥 6컵과 식초가루 2큰술을 섞어준 다음 볶아둔 당근, 우엉, 버섯을 넣고 고루 섞어 줍니다.

6 유부초밥을 만든 후 검은깨를 살짝 뿌려 접시에 담아 상에 냅니다.

Tip 시중에서 파는 조미된 유부를 구입하면 아주 편리합니다.

Fried bean curd pockets 유부

Sushi
초밥

4 Servings (24 pieces)

4 cups	Rice
3½ cups	Water
8 pieces	Salmon sashimi
8 pieces	Tuna sashimi
8 pieces	Yellow tail sashimi
1½ Tbsp	Vinegar powder

Dipping Sauce

TT*	Soy sauce
TT*	Wasabi

*TT : To Taste

Preparation

1 Rinse rice and drain water. Add water to rice in a medium-sized pot. Bring to a boil, stirring occasionally. Reduce heat to low and let simmer covered for 20 minutes. Turn off heat and let sit for another 10 minutes covered.

2 Combine steamed rice and vinegar powder in a large bowl. Let rice cool until lukewarm.

3 Wet hands and form bite-sized lumps of rice into oblong balls

4 Place a dab of wasabi on top of each rice ball. Arrange one piece of sashimi over each rice ball so that it drapes over the sides lengthwise.

5 Serve with soy sauce and wasabi.

Tip Cooked shrimp, cooked eel, or smoked salmon may be substituted for raw fish.

4 인분 (24개)

4 컵	쌀
3½ 컵	물
8 쪽	연어회
8 쪽	참치회
8 쪽	방어회
1½ 큰술	식초가루

찍어 먹는 소스
간장 적당량, 와사비 적당량

준비 과정

1 쌀을 깨끗이 씻어 물기를 완전히 뺀 후 중간 크기 냄비에 쌀과 분량의 물을 넣고 끓입니다. 밑이 눌지 않도록 수저로 저어줍니다. 끓기 시작하면 불을 약하게 줄이고 뚜껑을 닫아 20분 정도 끓입니다. 불을 끄고 뚜껑을 덮은 채로 10분 정도 둡니다.

2 밥에 식초가루를 뿌려 가볍게 섞은 후 식혀 둡니다.

3 밥이 완전히 식으면 먹기 좋은 크기로 뭉쳐서 접시에 담아줍니다.

4 와사비를 조금 덜어 뭉쳐 놓은 밥 위에 올리고 준비된 생선회감을 올려 초밥을 만듭니다.

5 와사비 간장을 옆에 곁들여 상에 냅니다. 식성에 따라 와사비는 필요한 만큼만 간장과 섞어 드시면 됩니다.

Tip 훈제 연어나 장어, 익은 새우를 사서 초밥을 만들면 날 생선을 먹지 않는 외국인들도 즐겨 먹습니다.

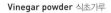

Vinegar powder 식초가루

Kimbop
김밥

4 Servings

4 cups	Steamed rice
2 Tbsp	Vinegar powder
1 bunch	Spinach
1	Carrot, julienned
4 oz.	Bulgogi beef (p.68)
2	Eggs, cooked into omelet and cut into 1/3-inch thick strips
4 pieces	Pickled radish, cut into 1/3-inch thick strips
4 sheets	Dried seaweed
TT*	Salt, sugar, sesame oil
As needed	Vegetable oil

*TT : To Taste

Preparation

1 Combine steamed rice and vinegar powder in a large bowl. Set aside.

2 Blanch spinach and squeeze out excess water. Toss spinach with salt and sesame oil. Set aside.

3 Heat vegetable oil in a large pan over medium-high heat. Add carrots and salt and sauté until carrots just become soft. Remove carrots and set aside.

4 Add oil to the same pan and cook bulgogi beef until desired doneness.

5 Take one sheet of dried seaweed and place on bamboo sushi mat. Evenly spread 1 cup of rice over the seaweed. Leave a 1-inch gap across one of the edges. Starting from the edge opposite the gap, place lines of spinach, pickled radish, beef, carrot, and egg over the rice. Starting again with the edge opposite the gap, roll the seaweed over the rice, beef and vegetables.

6 Slice the roll cross-wise into 1/2-inch pieces and serve with pickled radish.

4 인분

4 컵	밥
2 큰술	식초가루
1 단	시금치
1 개분	가늘게 채 썬 당근
115 g	불고기 (p.68)
2 개분	달걀지단
4 쪽	1 cm 두께로 길게 썬 단무지
4 장	김
적당량	소금, 설탕, 참기름
적당량	식용유

준비 과정

1 따뜻한 밥에 식초가루를 뿌려 식혀둡니다.

2 시금치는 깨끗이 씻어 뜨거운 물에 살짝 데친 후 물기를 꽉 짜서 소금과 참기름으로 무쳐 놓습니다.

3 곱게 채 썬 당근은 소금을 넣고 식용유에 볶습니다.

4 불고기 양념에 재놓은 고기는 프라이팬에 볶아둡니다.

5 김 발에 김을 깔고 김 끝의 2.5 cm 정도 남긴 부분까지 밥을 얇게 폅니다. 그 위에, 시금치, 단무지, 불고기, 당근, 달걀을 놓고 안에서 바깥쪽으로 말아줍니다.

6 먹기 좋은 크기로 썰어 단무지와 함께 상에 냅니다.

Pickled radish 단무지　**Seaweed** 김

Vegetable Wraps with Rice Ssambop
쌈밥정식

4 Servings

1	Boston lettuce
1	Radicchio
1	Lettuce
1	Bok choy
1	Endive lettuce
2	Hungarian peppers
4 cups	Steamed rice
As needed	Vegetable oil

Sauce

5 oz.	Pork, ground or chopped
1 Tbsp	Garlic, minced
3 Tbsp	Yellow onion, chopped
1 tsp	Ginger, minced
4 Tbsp	Soy bean paste
4 Tbsp	Red pepper paste
1 Tbsp	Sugar or corn syrup
1 Tbsp	Sesame seeds
3 Tbsp	Pine nuts, crushed
2 Tbsp	Sesame oil
TT*	Pepper
2	Green peppers, chopped (optional)
1 stalk	Scallion, chopped (optional)

* TT : To Taste

Preparation

1 Heat vegetable oil in large pan over medium-high heat and sauté pork, garlic, onion, and ginger. Add remaining sauce ingredients when the pork is fully cooked and stir for another minute. Turn off heat and add green peppers and scallion.

2 Arrange lettuce, radicchio, bok choy leaves, and Hungarian peppers and serve with sauce and steamed rice. Place rice and sauce inside one or more of the greens.

Tip For a meat option, wraps can be served with Bulgogi (p.68) or grilled spicy pork belly (p.84).

4 인분

1 개	보스턴 레터스
1 개	래디치오 양상추
1 개	적상추
1 개	청경채
1 개	엔다이브
2 개	헝가리 고추 (또는 풋고추)
4 컵	밥
적당량	식용유

쌈장
다진 돼지고기 140 g, 다진 마늘 1 큰술, 다진 양파 3 큰술,
다진 생강 1 작은술, 된장 4 큰술, 고추장 4 큰술,
설탕이나 물엿 1 큰술, 참깨 1 큰술, 잣가루 3 큰술,
참기름 2 큰술, 후추 적당량, 풋고추 2 개 (선택),
다진 파 1 줄기 (선택)

준비 과정

1 쌈장을 만들기 위해, 프라이팬에 식용유를 두르고 다진 돼지고기, 마늘, 양파, 생강을 넣고 볶다가 고기가 익으면 나머지 쌈장 재료를 넣고 같이 한 번 볶아줍니다. 풋고추와 파를 다져서 볶아준 양념에 섞고, 기호에 따라 참기름을 조금 더 넣어 쌈장을 준비합니다.

2 모든 야채는 깨끗이 씻어 채반에 밭쳐 물기를 뺀 후, 큰 접시에 보기 좋게 모양을 내서 놓고 쌈장을 곁들여 따뜻한 밥과 함께 상에 냅니다.

Tip 불고기(p.68 참조)나 삼겹살 고추장 구이 (p.84 참조)를 준비하여 같이 쌈을 싸 드시면 저녁 한 끼 식사로 좋습니다.

In Korean culinary tradition, noodles symbolize a long, healthy life. As a result, noodle dishes, though common in every-day meals, are often featured in holidays and celebrations.

한국 사람들은 잔칫날이면 국수요리를 내곤 한답니다. 국수발이 길기 때문인지 생일날 국수를 먹어야
오래 산다 하여 저희 어머니는 제 생일날이면 국수를 만들어 주곤 하셨습니다.

Noodles & Rice Cakes

국수와 떡볶이

Spicy Buckwheat Noodles
Jaengban Gooksu 쟁반국수

4 Servings

1 lb.	Chicken breast
TT*	Salt, pepper, white wine
2	Hard-boiled eggs, cut lengthwise into halves
9 oz.	Dried buckwheat noodles
2	Kirby cucumbers, julienned 1/4-inch long
1/2	Carrot, julienned 1/4-inch long
1/2	Asian pear, julienned 1/4-inch long
3 cups	Lettuce, chopped
5~6	Sesame leaves, julienned (optional)

Sauce

1 Tbsp	Soy sauce
2 Tbsp	Red pepper paste
2 Tbsp	Dried red pepper powder
3 Tbsp	Apple cider vinegar
1 tsp	Garlic, minced
1 Tbsp	Scallion, chopped
2 tsp	Korean mustard
1 Tbsp	Sesame oil
2 Tbsp	Brown sugar
1/2 cup	Sprite or other lime soda
1 Tbsp	Sesame seeds

*TT : To Taste

Preparation

1 Combine sauce ingredients in a medium-sized bowl. Set aside.

2 Rinse chicken breast in cold water and pat dry with paper towel. Season with salt and pepper and soak in white wine for 15 minutes. Bring water to a boil in a medium-sized pot over medium-high heat. Add chicken and cook for about 15-20 minutes or until chicken is cooked through. Remove chicken and let cool. Shred chicken breast into bite-sized strips.

3 Bring a medium-sized pot of water to a boil over medium-high heat. Add buckwheat noodles and cook to al dente. Remove and drain.

4 Arrange noodles, chicken, vegetables, and boiled eggs. Drizzle with sauce and sesame oil and garnish with sesame seeds. Serve immediately with extra sauce on the side.

Dried buckwheat noodles 메밀국수

4 인분

450 g	닭가슴살
적당량	소금, 후추, 화이트와인
2 개분	세로로 4분등한 삶은 달걀
250 g	메밀국수
2 개분	0.5cm로 채 썬 오이
1/2 개분	가늘게 채 썬 당근
1/2 개분	0.5cm로 채 썬 배
3 컵	2.5cm로 썬 상추
5~6 장분	가늘게 채 썬 깻잎 (선택)

매운 소스

간장 1 큰술, 고추장 2 큰술, 고춧가루 2 큰술,
사과 식초 3 큰술, 다진 마늘 1 작은술, 다진 파 1 큰술,
겨자 2 작은술, 참기름 1 큰술, 흑설탕 2 큰술,
사이다 1/2 컵, 참깨 1 큰술

준비 과정

1 매운 소스 재료를 한데 섞어둡니다.

2 깨끗이 씻은 닭가슴살은 소금과 후추로 간을 한 후, 화이트와인에 15분 정도 재두었다 끓는 물에 15~20분 정도 닭이 완전히 익을 때까지 삶아 줍니다. 다 익으면 건져내 식힌 후 먹기 좋은 크기로 길게 손으로 찢어줍니다.

3 끓는 물에 메밀국수를 삶아 건진 후 얼음물에 씻어 물기를 꽉 짜둡니다.

4 큰 쟁반에 닭가슴살과 야채, 달걀으로 모양을 내고 메밀국수는 돌돌 말아 놓습니다. 먹기 직전 소스를 넣어 섞고 참기름과 참깨를 한 번 살짝 더 뿌린 후 드시면 맛이 더 좋습니다.

Thin Noodle Soup
잔치국수

4~6 Servings

6 cups	Dried anchovy stock (p.235)
1 lb.	Dried thin noodles
4 oz.	Ground beef
1	Kirby cucumber, julienned
1	Egg, cooked into omelet and sliced thin
2 pieces	Dried seaweed, crushed
TT*	Salt, pepper, minced garlic
As needed	Vegetable oil

Seasoning

1 tsp	Soy sauce
1/2 tsp	Garlic, minced
1/2 tsp	Sugar
TT*	Salt, pepper

*TT : To Taste

Preparation

1 Bring dried anchovy stock to a boil in a large pot. Season with salt and pepper. Reduce heat to low and cover.

2 Bring water to a boil in another large pot over medium-high heat. Add noodles and cook to al dente. Remove noodles, rinse in cold water, and drain.

3 Combine beef with seasonings and cook in a pan over medium heat until cooked through. Remove beef, set aside, and wipe pan clean.

4 Heat vegetable oil in the same pan over medium heat. Add cucumbers, salt, pepper, and minced garlic and sauté until slightly soft.

5 Place noodles, beef, cucumbers, omelet slices, and crushed dried seaweed in individual serving bowls. Pour hot stock over noodles and serve.

4~6 인분

6컵	멸치 육수 (p,235)
450 g	소면
115 g	갈은 쇠고기
1 개분	채 썬 오이
1 개분	달걀지단
2장	부순 김
적당량	소금, 후추, 다진 마늘, 식용유

고기 양념

간장 1 작은술, 다진 마늘 1/2 작은술, 설탕 1/2 작은술,
소금 · 후추 적당량

준비 과정

1 멸치 육수는 소금, 후추로 간을 하여 한소끔 끓인 후 뚜껑을 닫고 약한 불에 올려둡니다.

2 끓는 물에 소면을 삶다가 끓어오르면 찬물을 한 컵 붓고 다시 끓어오르면 체에 밭쳐 찬물로 깨끗이 헹구어 둡니다.

3 고기는 양념에 무쳐 식용유를 두른 프라이팬에 고기가 다 익을 때까지 볶아둡니다.

4 채 썬 오이도 소금, 후추, 마늘을 넣고 기름에 살짝 볶아둡니다.

5 그릇에 소면을 담고 고기, 오이, 달걀지단, 부순 김을 올린 후 멸치 육수를 부어 상에 냅니다.

Thick Noodle Soup
Kal Gooksu 칼국수

4~6 Servings

1 lb.	Dried thick noodles
1	Korean zucchini, julienned
1	Carrot, julienned
1 tsp	Garlic, minced
2 pieces	Dried seaweed, julienned
6 cups	Dried anchovy stock (p.235)
8	Little neck clams
1 Tbsp	Soy sauce
TT*	Salt, pepper
As needed	Olive oil
As needed	Scallion, cut diagonally
As needed	Red pepper, cut diagonally

*TT : To Taste

Preparation

1 Bring water to a boil in a large pot over medium-high heat. Add noodles and cook to al dente. Drain noodles and set aside.

2 Heat olive oil in a medium-sized pan over medium-high heat. Add zucchini, carrots, salt, pepper, and 1 teaspoon of minced garlic and sauté until slightly soft.

3 Bring dried anchovy stock to a boil and season to taste with soy sauce, salt, and pepper. Add little neck clams and noodles and cook until noodles soften.

4 Remove noodles and clams and place in individual serving bowls with zucchini and carrots. Pour soup into each bowl and serve garnished with scallion, red pepper, and dried seaweed.

4~6 인분

450 g	칼국수
1 개분	채 썬 애호박
1 개분	채 썬 당근
1 작은술	다진 마늘
2 장	채 썬 김
6 컵	멸치 육수 (p.235)
8 개	바지락조개
1 큰술	간장
적당량	소금, 후추
적당량	올리브오일
적당량	어슷 썬 파 · 어슷 썬 홍고추

준비 과정

1 끓는 물에 국수를 삶다가 끓어오르면 찬물을 한 컵 붓고, 다시 끓어오를 때 국수가 거의 다 익은 듯 하면 건져 체에 밭쳐 둡니다.

2 애호박과 당근은 소금, 후추, 마늘 1작은술과 함께 식용유에 볶아둡니다.

3 멸치 육수를 끓여 간장, 소금, 후추로 간을 하고 조개를 넣어 한소끔 끓인 후 삶아 놓은 국수를 넣고 한 번 끓어오르면 불을 끕니다.

4 그릇에 국수와 조개를 담고 호박, 당근, 어슷 썬 파와 홍고추를 올리고 육수를 부은 다음 김을 올려서 상에 냅니다.

Chilled Buckwheat Noodle Soup

Mulnaengmyun 물냉면

4 Servings

1 lb.	Beef brisket
12 cups	Water
5 cloves	Garlic, peeled
1 oz.	Ginger, peeled
1	Yellow onion
1 tsp	Peppercorns
2	Kirby cucumbers, cut diagonally
1	Asian pear, sliced thin
2	Hard-boiled eggs, cut lengthwise into 4 pieces
1 lb.	Korean buckwheat noodles
TT*	Sugar, salt, vinegar, Korean mustard

*TT : To Taste

Preparation

1 Soak beef brisket in cold water for 20 minutes. Remove and rinse.

2 Bring brisket, garlic, ginger, onion, peppercorns, and 12 cups of water to a boil in a large pot. Reduce heat to low and simmer for 1 hour. Skim surface residue. Remove brisket and set aside.

3 Strain stock and add 1 tablespoon of sugar. Set aside covered in refrigerator.

4 Soak cucumbers in sweet vinegar water (equal parts sugar, salt, and vinegar) for at least 1 hour. Remove and squeeze out excess liquid.

5 Bring a big pot of water to a boil. Add noodles and cook for 1~2 minutes. Remove noodles, rinse in cold water, and drain.

6 Place noodles in individual serving bowls. Arrange a few slices of brisket, cucumbers, pear, and 1 piece of hard-boiled egg over the noodles. Pour cold beef stock over noodles and serve with Korean mustard and vinegar.

4 인분

450 g	양지머리
12 컵	물
5 쪽	마늘
30 g	생강
1 개	양파
1 작은술	통후추
2 개분	어슷 썬 오이
1 개분	얇게 저민 배
2 개분	4등분한 삶은 달걀
450 g	냉면 국수(냉장)
적당량	설탕, 소금, 식초, 겨자

준비 과정

1 양지머리는 20분 정도 찬물에 담가 핏물을 뺀 다음 잘 씻어줍니다.

2 물 12컵에 고기, 마늘, 생강, 양파, 통후추를 넣고 끓이다 불을 줄여 1시간 정도 끓이면서 위에 뜨는 찌꺼기와 기름은 제거합니다.

3 1시간 후 고기는 꺼내 편육을 준비하고, 국물은 체에 밭친 다음 설탕 1큰술과 잘 섞은 후 소금으로 간을 하여 랩을 씌워 냉장고에 차갑게 보관합니다.

4 오이는 단촛물(설탕 : 소금 : 식초 1 : 1 : 1)에 1시간 정도 담가 뒀다 물기를 꼭 짜둡니다.

5 끓는 물에 냉면국수를 1~2분 정도 삶아낸 후 찬물에 비벼 씻어 체에 밭쳐 둡니다.

6 큰 그릇에 냉면국수를 넣고 고기, 오이, 배, 달걀을 올린 다음 차가운 육수를 붓고 겨자와 식초를 함께 상에 냅니다.

Spicy Buckwheat Noodles

Bibim Naengmyun 비빔냉면

4 Servings

8 oz.	Beef, ground
8 oz.	Radish, sliced thin
2	Cucumbers, cut diagonally crosswise
1	Asian pear, julienned
2	Hard-boiled eggs, cut lengthwise into 4 pieces
1 lb.	Korean buckwheat noodles

Seasoning

2 tsp	Soy sauce
1 tsp	Garlic, minced
1 tsp	Sugar
TT*	Salt, pepper

Sauce

6 Tbsp	Red pepper paste
2 Tbsp	Dried red pepper powder
6 Tbsp	Vinegar
2 tsp	Garlic, minced
4 Tbsp	Scallion, chopped
2 Tbsp	Sugar
As needed	Sugar, salt, vinegar, and water

Preparation

1 Combine sauce ingredients in a small bowl. Set aside.

2 Combine ground beef with seasonings in a medium sized-bowl. Heat vegetable oil in a medium-sized pan over medium-high heat. Add beef and cook until well browned.

3 Soak radish in sweet vinegar water (equal parts sugar, salt, vinegar, and water) for at least 1 hour. Remove and squeeze at excess liquid.

4 Bring water to a boil in a large pot over medium-high heat. Add buckwheat noodles and cook for 1~2 minutes. Remove and rinse in cold water.

5 Arrange noodles, beef, pickled radish, cucumbers, pear, and 1 piece of egg in individual serving bowls. Serve with sauce on the side.

4인분

225 g	갈은 쇠고기
225 g	저며 썬 무
2 개분	어슷 썬 오이
1 개분	채 썬 배
2 개분	4등분한 삶은 달걀
450 g	냉면 국수(냉장)

쇠고기 양념

간장 2 작은술, 다진 마늘 1 작은술, 설탕 1 작은술, 소금 · 후추 적당량

비빔냉면 소스

고추장 6 큰술, 고춧가루 2 큰술, 식초 6 큰술, 다진 마늘 2 작은술, 다진 파 4 큰술, 설탕 2 큰술

단촛물

설탕 · 소금 · 식초 · 물 적당량

준비과정

1 비빔 냉면 소스를 한데 섞어둡니다.

2 갈은 쇠고기를 양념에 잘 버무려 식용유를 두른 프라이팬에 볶습니다.

3 얇게 저며 썬 무를 단촛물(설탕 · 소금 · 식초 · 물 같은 양)에 1시간 정도 담가뒀다 먹기 좋은 크기로 썰어 냉면 무를 준비합니다.

4 끓는 물에 냉면을 넣어 1~2분 정도 삶은 다음 꺼내 차가운 물에 손으로 비벼가면서 헹궈둡니다.

5 큰 그릇에 냉면국수, 볶은 고기, 냉면 무, 오이, 배를 담고 4등분한 삶은 달걀 한쪽을 위에 올려 줍니다. 비빔냉면 소스를 볼에 잘 섞어 냉면과 함께 상에 냅니다.

Noodles with Black Bean Sauce

Jajang Myun 자장면

4~6 Servings

1 ½ lb.	Dried thick noodles
1/2 lb.	Pork belly, cut into bite-sized pieces
1/2 tsp	Garlic, minced
1/2 tsp	Ginger, minced
1	Onion, cut into small cubes
1	Idaho potato, cut into small cubes
1	Zucchini, cut into small cubes
1	Cucumber, julienned
As needed	Vegetable oil

Sauce

6 Tbsp	Roasted black bean sauce
1 Tbsp	Miso (optional)
1/2 Tbsp	Sugar
2 Tbsp	Red wine
5 Tbsp	Water
4 Tbsp	Corn starch and water (1:4 ratio)

Preparation

1 Bring water to a boil in a large pot over medium-high heat. Add noodles and cook to al dente. Remove noodles, rinse in cold water, and drain. Set aside.

2 Combine black bean sauce ingredients (except for corn starch water) in a bowl and set aside.

3 Heat vegetable oil in a medium-sized pan over medium heat. Add garlic and ginger and sauté until lightly browned. Add pork belly and sauté until pork turns color. Add onion, potato, and zucchini and sauté for another 10~15 minutes or until pork is cooked through.

4 Add black bean sauce and simmer for 3~5 minutes. Slowly add corn starch water while stirring and simmer for another 3~5 minutes.

5 Place noodles in individual serving bowls and pour black bean sauce over the top. Serve garnished with cucumbers.

4~6 인분

675 g	우동 국수
225 g	한 입 크기로 썬 돼지고기 삼겹살
1/2 작은술	다진 마늘
1/2 작은술	다진 생강
1 개분	작게 깍둑 썬 양파
1 개분	작게 깍둑 썬 감자
1 개분	작게 깍둑 썬 호박
1 개분	채 썬 오이
적당량	식용유

자장 소스

볶은 자장 6 큰술, 미소 된장 (선택) 1 큰술,
설탕 1/2 큰술, 레드와인 2 큰술, 물 5 큰술,
녹말물 (녹말과 물의 비율 1:4) 4 큰술

준비 과정

1 우동 국수는 끓는 물에 넣어 다 익을때까지 삶은 후 찬물에 헹궜다 물기를 빼둡니다.

2 녹말물을 제외한 자장 소스 재료를 한데 섞어 준비합니다.

3 프라이팬에 식용유를 두르고 마늘, 생강을 볶다가 돼지고기를 넣고 고기가 다 익은 듯하면 양파, 감자, 호박을 넣고 10~15분 정도 볶아줍니다.

4 고기와 야채를 볶은 프라이팬에 자장 소스를 넣어 끓이면서 좀 더 볶아 준 다음, 녹말물을 천천히 부어 넣고 3~5분 정도 더 끓이면서 잘 저어줍니다.

5 그릇에 국수를 담고 자장 소스를 올린 후 채 썬 오이로 장식해서 상에 냅니다.

Spicy Seafood Noodles Jjampong

짬뽕

4 Servings

1½ lb.	Dried thick noodles
8 oz.	Shrimp, peeled and cleaned
4 oz.	Mussels, meat only
4 oz.	Squid, body only
1/2 lb.	Pork loin, sliced thin
1 Tbsp	White wine
1 Tbsp	Soy sauce
TT*	Pepper
2 Tbsp	Red pepper oil
2 Tbsp	Chili sauce
1/2 tsp	Garlic, minced
1/2 tsp	Ginger, minced
1	Yellow onion, sliced
1/2	Carrot, sliced
4	Shitake mushrooms, sliced
1/2 cup	Large green onion, sliced
3 Tbsp	Soy sauce
2 Tbsp	White wine
8 cups	Chicken stock

*TT : To Taste

Preparation

1 Rinse squid and slice into bite-sized pieces. Set aside.

2 Combine pork with white wine, soy sauce, and pepper. Let marinate for at least 10 minutes.

3 Heat red pepper oil in a large pot over medium heat. Add chili sauce, minced garlic, and ginger and cook until lightly browned. Add pork, onion, carrots, shitake mushrooms, and large green onion and sauté for 2~3 minutes. Season with soy sauce and white wine to taste.

4 Add chicken stock and bring to a boil over high heat. Add shrimp, mussels, and squid and cook for another 3~4 minutes. Season with salt and pepper.

5 Bring a separate pot of water to a boil and cook noodles until soft. Remove noodles and rinse in cold water.

6 Place noodles in individual serving bowls and ladle in soup, seafood, and vegetables. Serve hot.

Tip Add a few drops of vinegar and/or chopped basil.

4 인분

675g	굵은 국수
225g	새우
115g	홍합
115g	오징어
225g	돼지고기
1 큰술	화이트와인
1 큰술	간장
적당량	후추

짬뽕 국물
고추기름 2 큰술, 칠리 소스 2 큰술, 다진 마늘 1/2 작은술,
다진 생강 1/2 작은술, 채 썬 양파 1 개분, 채 썬 당근 1/2 개분,
채 썬 표고버섯 4 개, 채 썬 대파 1/2 컵, 간장 3 큰술,
화이트와인 2 큰술, 닭 육수 8 컵

준비 과정

1 오징어는 깨끗이 씻어서 먹기 좋은 크기로 썰어둡니다.

2 돼지고기는 채 썰어서 화이트와인과 간장, 후추에 10분 정도 재둡니다.

3 큰 냄비에 고추기름을 두르고 칠리소스, 마늘, 생강을 넣고 잠깐 볶다가 고기, 양파, 당근, 표고버섯, 대파를 넣고 2~3분 정도 볶은 후 간장과 화이트와인으로 맛을 냅니다.

4 닭 육수를 부어 넣고 한소끔 끓으면 새우, 홍합, 오징어를 넣고 3~4분 정도 끓이다 소금과 후추로 간을 합니다.

5 끓는 물에 굵은 국수를 삶아 익으면 꺼내 찬물에 헹군 후 물기를 빼둡니다.

6 큰 그릇에 국수를 담고 준비한 짬뽕 국물을 부어 상에 냅니다. 뜨겁게 데운 국물을 부어 드셔야 제 맛이 납니다.

Tip 식초를 약간 떨어뜨려 섞어 드셔도 맛이 좋습니다. 바질을 잘게 다져 올리면 색다른 맛을 냅니다.

Thick noodles 생국수
Dried noodles 마른 국수

Cold Noodles with Kimchi
김치 비빔국수

4 Servings

3 bundles	Dried thin noodles
2 cups	Ripe kimchi, chopped rough
2	Kirby cucumbers, julienned
8 oz.	Ham, julienned
2	Hard-boiled eggs, cut into halves
TT*	Sesame oil, sesame seeds

Sauce

2 Tbsp	Red pepper paste
1 Tbsp	Soy sauce
2 Tbsp	Sugar
1 Tbsp	Apple cider vinegar
1 Tbsp	Dried red pepper powder
1/2 tsp	Garlic, minced
3 Tbsp	Scallion, chopped
1 Tbsp	Sesame oil
1 Tbsp	Sesame seeds
TT*	Salt, pepper

*TT : To Taste

Preparation

1 Combine sauce ingredients in a small bowl. Set aside.

2 Bring noodles to a boil in a medium-sized pot over medium-high heat. Cook until soft. Remove noodles, rinse with ice cold water, and drain.

3 Combine kimchi with sesame oil and sesame seeds.

4 Mix noodles, kimchi, cucumber, and ham with the sauce. Serve garnished with cucumbers and boiled eggs.

Tip Boiled beef or chicken can be substituted for ham.

4 인분

3 묶음	소면
2 컵	잘게 썬 익은 김치
2 개분	채 썬 오이
225 g	채 썬 햄
2 개분	삶은 달걀
적당량	참기름, 참깨

비빔 양념

고추장 2 큰술, 간장 1 큰술 , 설탕 2 큰술, 사과식초 1 큰술,
고춧가루 1 큰술, 다진 마늘 1/2 작은술, 다진 파 3 큰술,
참기름 1 큰술, 참깨 1 큰술, 소금 · 후추 적당량

준비 과정

1 소스 재료를 한데 섞어둡니다.

2 끓는 물에 국수를 넣고 끓어오르면 찬물 한 컵을 붓고 다시 끓어오르면 빨리 얼음물에 넣어 건져서 체에 밭쳐둡니다.

3 송송 썰은 김치는 참기름과 참깨로 살짝 버무려 둡니다.

4 국수에 김치, 오이, 햄을 넣고 소스에 버무린 후 오이채와 달걀을 올려 상에 냅니다.

Tip 햄 대신 쇠고기나 닭을 삶아 사용해도 좋습니다.

Spicy Rice Finger Cakes Dukboki
고추장 떡볶이

4 Servings

1½ lb.	Rice finger cakes
1/2 lb.	Fish cake
1 stalk	Scallion, cut diagonally

Sauce

2 cups	Dried anchovy stock (p.235)
4 Tbsp	Red pepper paste
1 Tbsp	Dried red pepper powder
2 Tbsp	Sugar
1 Tbsp	Garlic, minced
TT*	Salt

*TT : To Taste

Preparation

1 Soak rice finger cakes in water for 20~30 minutes. Drain water.

2 Cut fish cake into triangle slices. Place in boiling water for 1~2 minutes.

3 Combine sauce ingredients in a bowl. Pour sauce ingredients in a large pan over medium-high heat and bring to a light boil.

4 Add rice cakes, reduce heat to low, and simmer until rice finger cakes are soft. Add fish cake slices and simmer until rice cakes are cooked. Add scallion and turn off heat.

5 Serve immediately.

4 인분

680 g	떡볶이 떡
230 g	어묵
1 줄기분	어슷 썬 파

양념

멸치 육수 2 컵(p.235), 고추장 4 큰술, 고춧가루 1 큰술, 설탕 2 큰술, 다진 마늘 1 큰술, 소금 적당량

준비 과정

1 떡볶이 떡을 물에 20~30분 정도 담가두었다가 물을 따라내고 준비합니다.

2 어묵은 세모 모양으로 잘라 끓는 물에 1~2분 정도 살짝 데쳐둡니다.

3 떡볶이 양념을 한데 섞은 후 프라이팬에 끓입니다.

4 떡볶이 떡을 넣고 반쯤 익으면 데친 어묵을 넣어 섞어줍니다. 떡이 익으면 파를 넣고 불을 끕니다.

5 뜨거울 때 접시에 담아 상에 냅니다.

Traditional Rice Finger Cakes
궁중 떡볶이

4~6 Servings

1 lb.	Rice finger cakes
4 oz.	Beef, sliced
4 oz.	Shitake mushrooms, sliced
4 oz.	Carrot, julienned
1/2	Onion, sliced
1	Egg, cooked into omelet and sliced thick
As needed	Olive oil, sesame oil, soy sauce

Sauce

2 Tbsp	Soy sauce
1 Tbsp	Scallion, chopped
1 tsp	Garlic, minced
2 tsp	Sugar
2 tsp	Sesame oil
2 tsp	Sesame seeds
TT*	Salt, pepper

*TT : To Taste

Preparation

1 Bring water to a boil in a large pot. Add rice finger cakes and cook for 1~2 minutes. Drain water and leave rice cakes in the pot. Add 1 teaspoon olive oil, 1 teaspoon sesame oil, and 2 teaspoons soy sauce and set aside.

2 Combine sauce ingredients in a large bowl. Add beef and onion to half the sauce and let sit for a few minutes.

3 Heat olive oil in a large pan over high heat. Add beef and onion and cook for 3~4 minutes. Add carrots and mushrooms halfway through.

4 Add rice finger cakes and remaining sauce and cook for another 4~5 minutes. Garnish with egg omelet slices and serve immediately.

4~6 인분

450 g	떡볶이 떡
120 g	채 썬 쇠고기
120 g	채 썬 표고버섯
120 g	채 썬 당근
1/2 개분	채 썬 양파
1 개분	달걀지단
적당량	올리브오일, 참기름

소스

간장 2 큰술, 다진 파 1 큰술, 다진 마늘 1 작은술,
설탕 2 작은술, 참기름 2 작은술, 참깨 2 작은술,
올리브오일 · 참기름 · 소금 적당량

준비 과정

1 떡볶이 떡은 뜨거운 물에 살짝 데쳐서 물기를 빼고 건져낸 후, 올리브오일 1작은술과 참기름 1작은술, 간장 2작은술을 섞어 버무려 둡니다.

2 절반의 양념에 고기와 양파를 버무린 후 간이 배도록 잠시 둡니다.

3 달궈진 프라이팬에 올리브오일을 두르고 고기와 양파를 3~4분 정도 볶다가 당근과 버섯을 넣고 볶습니다.

4 고기와 야채를 볶다 떡볶이 떡과 나머지 양념을 모두 넣고 4~5분 정도 같이 볶아줍니다. 달걀지단으로 모양을 내 뜨거울 때 상에 냅니다.

As mentioned earlier, Korean meals do not typically include Western style salads. Rather, vegetables are featured more prominently in the form of a variety of side dishes collectively called banchan. A Korean meal can feature anywhere from three to over a dozen banchan dishes, which can provide even the most basic meals with a variety of flavors and textures.

한국인들의 식사에는 반찬이 상에 많이 오른답니다. 5~12가지까지 다양한 반찬을 올려 고루고루 영양가 있는 음식을 접하곤 하지요. 그래서 주부들은 반찬을 골고루 준비해 냉장고에 넣어두었다 식사 때마다 다른 반찬을 상에 올리곤 합니다.

Sides

반찬

Kimchi 포기김치

Radish Kimchi Kagdoogee 깍두기

Sweet Kimchi Mul Kimchi 물김치

Spicy Napa Cabbage and Oysters 배추 겉절이

Cucumber Kimchi Oy Kimchi 오이소박이

Walnut Anchovies 호두 멸치 볶음

Soy Sauce Beef Jangjorim 장조림

Marinated Squid 오징어젓

Spicy Oysters 어리굴젓

Seasoned Spinach · Bean Sprouts · Cucumbers 시금치나물, 콩나물 무침, 오이나물

Kimchi

포기김치

10 Servings

6 lb.	Napa cabbage
1 cup	Salt

Kimchi Stuffing

4 lb.	Korean radish, julienned
1 cup	Dried red pepper powder
1 cup	Salted anchovy sauce
2 Tbsp	Garlic, minced
2 Tbsp	Yellow onion, pureed
1 Tbsp	Ginger, minced
1	Apple, pureed
1 stalk	Scallion, cut diagonally
2 Tbsp	Salt
1 Tbsp	Sugar
TT*	Salt

*TT : To Taste

Preparation

1 Rinse cabbage and drain. Cut cabbage lengthwise into 6 pieces. Sprinkle 1 cup of salt in between leaves and let sit for 6~7 hours.

2 Toss julienned radish with dried red pepper powder. Let sit for 30 minutes. Add anchovy sauce, garlic, ginger, apple, scallion, salt, and sugar to make stuffing.

3 Rinse salted cabbage and squeeze out excess water. Liberally stuff cabbage leaves with stuffing. Fold in halves and place in a jar. Pack cabbage in well.

4 Store jar at room temperature for 1 day. Refrigerate for at least 1 week before serving.

10 인분

2,8 kg	배추 한 포기
1 컵	소금

김치속

1,8 kg	무
1 컵	고춧가루
1 컵	멸치액젓
2 큰술	다진 마늘
2 큰술	양파즙
1 큰술	다진 생강
1 개분	사과즙
1 줄기분	어슷 썬 파
2 큰술	소금
1 큰술	설탕
적당량	소금

준비 과정

1 배추를 깨끗이 씻어 물기를 제거한 후 세로로 6등분합니다. 소금 1컵을 배춧잎 사이사이에 뿌린 후 6~7시간 동안 절여둡니다.

2 무는 채 썰어 고춧가루를 넣어 30분 정도 무에 물이 들도록 둡니다. 여기에 멸치액젓, 마늘, 생강, 간 사과, 파, 소금과 설탕을 넣고 김치 속을 준비합니다.

3 절여진 배추를 깨끗이 씻어 물기를 짠 후 준비된 속을 사이사이 넣어줍니다. 속을 넣은 배추는 반으로 접어 통에 담아 꾸욱 눌러줍니다.

4 하루 정도 실온에 익힌 다음 냉장고에 일주일 정도 두었다 드시면 됩니다.

Salted Napa cabbage 절인 배추

Napa cabbage 배추

Radish Kimchi Kagdoogee

깍두기

10 Servings

5 lb.	Korean radish, peeled, ends removed
2 Tbsp	Salt
1 Tbsp	Sugar

Seasoning

4 cup	Dried red pepper powder
1 Tbsp	Sugar
3 Tbsp	Garlic, minced
1 tsp	Ginger, minced
1 Tbsp	Pear, pureed (optional)
1/2 cup	Scallion, cut diagonally
5 Tbsp	Salted anchovy sauce or fish sauce

Preparation

1 Cut radish into 3/4-inch cubes and toss with 1 tablespoon sugar and 2 tablespoons salt in a medium-sized bowl. Let sit for 1 hour. Remove radish and set aside remaining juice.

2 Season radish with dried red pepper powder. Let sit for about 30 minutes. Add sugar, garlic, ginger, pear, scallion, and 4 tablespoons of anchovy sauce. Toss well.

3 Place radish, remaining anchovy sauce, and radish juice in a jar. Pack radish in well.

4 Seal jar and store at room temperature for one day. Refrigerate for at least 1 week before serving.

Tip Salted anchovy sauce brands have varying salt content, so add more or less sauce as needed.

10 인분

2.25 kg	무
2 큰술	소금
1 큰술	설탕

양념

4 컵	고춧가루
1 큰술	설탕
2 ½ 큰술	다진 마늘
1 작은술	다진 생강
1 큰술	배즙(선택)
1/2	어슷 썬 파
5 큰술	멸치액젓 또는 피시소스

준비 과정

1 무를 2cm 크기로 깍둑 썰어 설탕 1큰술과 소금 2큰술에 1시간 정도 절여 둡니다. 무는 건져 내고 무에서 빠진 즙은 따로 둡니다.

2 무에 고춧가루를 넣고 버무려 30분 정도 둬 빨갛게 물이 들면, 멸치액젓 4큰술과 설탕, 다진 마늘, 생강, 배즙을 넣고 버무린 후 어슷 썬 파를 넣고 다시 살짝 버무립니다.

3 따로 둔 무즙에 나머지 멸치액젓 1큰술을 섞은 다음 유리병에 무를 담고 무즙과 액젓 섞은 물을 부어주고 꾹꾹 눌러줍니다.

4 하루 정도 실온에 두었다 일주일 정도 냉장고에서 익게 하여 꺼내 드시면 좋습니다.

Tip 멸치액젓에 따라 소금 양이 틀리니 액젓 양을 조절하여 사용해야 됩니다.

Korean radish 무

Sweet Kimchi Mul Kimchi
물김치

8~10 Servings

12 cups	Water
4 Tbsp	Salt
4 Tbsp	Sugar
4 cups	Napa cabbage, cut into bite-sized pieces
2 cups	Korean radish, cut into bite-sized pieces
3 stalks	Scallion, cut into 1-inch pieces
1 pack	Korean watercress (optional), cut into 1-inch pieces
4 cloves	Garlic, sliced thin
1 tsp	Ginger, sliced thin
1 Tbsp	Dried red pepper powder
1	Apple, cut lengthwise into 4 pieces
As needed	Pine nuts

Preparation

1 Dissolve salt and sugar in 12 cups of water in a jar. Add cabbage, radish, scallion and Korean watercress.

2 Wrap garlic and ginger in cheese cloth and place in jar.

3 Wrap 1 tablespoon of dried red pepper powder in cheesecloth and place in jar. Squeeze red pepper pouch inside jar periodically and discard after 30 minutes.

4 Seal jar and store in a cool, dark room for one day. Remove garlic and ginger pouch and add apples.

5 Refrigerate for at least 3~4 days before serving. Serve garnished with pine nuts.

Tip Garlic, ginger, and red pepper powder may be added directly if cheese cloth is unavailable.

8~10 인분

12 컵	물
4 큰술	소금
4 큰술	설탕
4 컵	먹기 좋게 썬 배추
2 컵	먹기 좋게 썬 무
3 줄기	2.5 cm 길이로 썬 파
1 단	2.5 cm 길이로 썬 미나리
4 쪽분	채 썬 마늘
1 작은술	채 썬 생강
1 큰술	고춧가루
1 개분	4등분한 사과
적당량	잣

준비 과정

1 물 12컵에 소금과 설탕을 넣고 잘 섞어 녹입니다. 병에 썰어놓은 배추와 무, 파, 미나리를 넣고, 준비된 소금과 설탕 섞은 물을 부어 넣습니다.

2 마늘 채와 생강 채는 거즈에 싸서 넣습니다.

3 다른 거즈에 고춧가루 1큰술을 넣고 잘 묶은 후 병 속에 넣고 30분 정도 담가 두면 빨간 고춧물이 나옵니다. 중간중간 한 번씩 손으로 꽉 짜준 다음 30분 후에 꺼내서 버립니다.

4 병을 어둡고 선선한 장소에 하루쯤 두었다가 마늘과 생강을 싼 거즈는 건져 버리고 4등분한 사과를 넣습니다.

5 냉장고에 3~4일 정도 넣어 두었다 꺼내 그릇에 담고 잣을 올려 상에 냅니다.

Tip 고춧가루를 거즈에 싸서 병에 넣으면 깨끗한 김치국물을 만들 수 있습니다. 이것이 번거롭다면 그냥 고춧가루를 넣어도 됩니다.

Spicy Napa Cabbage and Oysters
배추 겉절이

4 Servings

1 lb.	Napa cabbage
3 Tbsp	Salt
1 cup	Water
8 oz.	Oysters, removed from shells
1 Tbsp	Sesame seeds
TT*	Salt, pepper
2 stalk	Scallion, cut diagonally

Seasoning

2 Tbsp	Dried red pepper powder
2 Tbsp	Sugar
1 Tbsp	Fish sauce
2 Tbsp	Scallion, chopped
1 Tbsp	Garlic, minced
1/2 tsp	Ginger, minced
1 tsp	Sesame oil

Preparation

1 Soak Napa cabbage in salt water (3 tablespoons salt to 1 cup water) for 30 minutes. Remove cabbage, rinse, and drain. Cut cabbage lengthwise into slices.

2 Rinse oysters in salt water.

3 Combine seasoning ingredients in a large bowl. Add cabbage and oysters and toss well.

4 Serve immediately garnished with sesame seeds and scallion.

4 인분

450 g	배추
3 큰술	소금
1 컵	물
225 g	굴
1 큰술	참깨
적당량	소금, 후추
2 줄기	어슷 썬 파

양념

고춧가루 2 큰술, 설탕 2 큰술, 피시소스 1 큰술,
다진 파 2 큰술, 다진 마늘 1 큰술, 다진 생강 1/2 작은술,
참기름 1 작은술

준비 과정

1 배추는 소금물(소금 3 큰술 : 물 1 컵)에 30분 정도 절인 다음 깨끗이 씻어 체에 밭쳐 물기가 빠지면 길이로 썰어 놓습니다.

2 굴은 소금물에 헹구어 깨끗이 씻어 둡니다.

3 양념 재료를 한데 섞은 후 배추를 넣어 잘 버무리고 나서 굴을 넣고 살짝 버무립니다.

4 접시에 담고 참깨와 어슷 썬 파를 올려 장식한 후 상에 냅니다.

Cucumber Kimchi Oy Kimchi
오이소박이

4 Servings

5	Cucumbers, ends removed
2 Tbsp	Salt
2 cups	Water
1 cup	Korean chives, chopped
1/2 cup	Carrots, julienned 1/2-inch long
1 Tbsp	Scallions, chopped

Seasoning

1 Tbsp	Fish sauce
2 Tbsp	Dried red pepper powder
1/2 tsp	Garlic, minced
1 tsp	Sesame seeds
1 tsp	Sugar

Preparation

1 Cut cucumbers crosswise in halves and then lengthwise into quarters, stopping just before cutting all the way through. Soak in salt water (2 tablespoons salt to 2 cups water) for 30 minutes. Drain water and set aside.

2 Combine seasoning ingredients in a large bowl. Add chives, carrots, and scallion and toss well.

3 Stuff mixture into the slots cut into the cucumbers. Place stuffed cucumbers in a jar.

4 Add 2~3 tablespoons of water to the seasoning left in the bowl and pour into jar. Refrigerate for 1 or 2 days before serving.

4 인분

5 개	오이
2 큰술	소금
2 컵	물
1 컵	다진 부추
1/2 컵	1cm로 채 썬 당근
1 큰술	다진 파

양념
피시소스 1 큰술, 고춧가루 2 큰술, 다진 마늘 1/2 작은술, 참깨 1 작은술, 설탕 1 작은술

준비 과정

1 오이는 양 끝부분을 잘라내고 가로로 반을 자른 후 십자가 모양으로 끝부분이 떨어지지 않게 세로로 자릅니다. 소금물 (소금 2큰술 : 물 2컵)에 오이를 30분 정도 담갔다 건져 둡니다.

2 양념 재료를 한데 섞은 후 부추, 당근, 파를 넣고 무쳐 놓습니다.

3 준비된 오이 속을 무쳐 놓은 양념으로 채운 후 병에 담습니다.

4 양념을 섞은 그릇에 물 2~3큰술을 부어 오이를 채운 병에 붓습니다. 하루나 이틀 정도 냉장고에 넣고 익혀 드셔야 좋습니다.

Walnut Anchovies
호두 멸치 볶음

4~6 Servings

1 cup	Dried small anchovies
1 cup	Walnuts, chopped
As needed	Vegetable oil
1 Tbsp	Honey or corn syrup
TT*	Sesame seeds

4~6 인분

1 컵	잔멸치
1 컵	호두
적당량	식용유
1 큰술	꿀이나 물엿
적당량	참깨

Preparation

1 Heat vegetable oil in a medium-sized pan over medium heat. Add anchovies and sauté for 5~6 minutes.

2 Add walnuts and cook for another 3 minutes. Add honey or corn syrup and cook for another 3~4 minutes. Remove from heat and let cool

3 Serve garnished with sesame seeds.

준비 과정

1 중불 프라이팬에 기름을 넉넉히 두르고 잘 다듬어진 멸치를 5~6분간 볶아줍니다.

2 호두를 넣고 3분 정도 볶다가 꿀이나 물엿을 넣고 3~4분 정도 볶아준 후 불을 끄고 식힙니다.

3 참깨를 뿌려 상에 냅니다.

Soy Sauce Beef Jangjorim

장조림

4~6 Servings

1 lb.	Beef flank
5	Green peppers
15 cloves	Garlic, peeled
1 oz.	Ginger
5 cups	Water
3/4 cup	Soy sauce
1 Tbsp	Sugar
5	Hard-boiled eggs

Preparation

1 Bring beef, 5 cloves of garlic, ginger, and 5 cups of water to a boil in a large pot over high heat. Reduce heat and simmer covered for 1 hour. Skim surface residue and discard garlic and ginger.

2 Add remaining garlic, green peppers, soy sauce, and sugar. Bring to a boil and turn off heat.

3 Remove beef, cut into 8 pieces, and place in a jar with boiled eggs, green peppers, garlic, and reduced liquid. Keep stored in refrigerator.

4 Serve beef and eggs together.

4~6 인분

450 g	장조림용 쇠고기
5개	꽈리고추
15 쪽	마늘
30 g	생강
5 컵	물
3/4 컵	간장
1 큰술	설탕
5개	삶은 달걀

준비 과정

1 큰 냄비에 쇠고기와 마늘 5개, 생강을 넣고 끓기 시작하면 중불로 줄여서 1시간가량 뚜껑을 덮고 끓입니다. 중간중간 찌꺼기를 걸러줍니다. 마늘과 생강은 건져냅니다.

2 나머지 마늘 10개와 꽈리고추, 간장, 설탕을 넣고 한소끔 끓으면 불을 끕니다.

3 고기는 꺼내 먹기 좋은 크기로 8등분 정도로 잘라 삶은 달걀, 꽈리고추, 마늘, 끓인 간장과 함께 병에 담아 냉장고에 넣어둡니다.

4 손으로 고기를 가늘게 찢어 달걀과 함께 반찬으로 드시면 좋습니다.

Marinated Squid
오징어젓

8~10 Servings

2	Large squid, body only
3 Tbsp	Squid sauce
1 lb.	Korean radish
TT*	Salt

Seasoning
4 Tbsp	Dried red pepper powder
5 Tbsp	Squid sauce
3 Tbsp	Sugar
2 Tbsp	Garlic, minced
2 tsp	Ginger, minced

*TT : To Taste

Preparation

1 Combine seasoning ingredients in a large bowl. Set aside.

2 Clean squid and blot dry with paper towel. Cut squid into 1/4 × 2-inch pieces. Marinate squid in squid sauce for 3 hours.

3 Cut radish into 1/4 × 2-inch pieces. Season with salt and let sit for 30 minutes.

4 Add squid and radish to seasoning and toss well. Place mixture in a jar and store in refrigerator for 5~7 days before serving.

8~10 인분

2 마리	오징어
3 큰술	오징어 액젓
450 g	무
적당량	소금

양념
고춧가루 4 큰술, 오징어 액젓 5 큰술, 설탕 3 큰술,
다진 마늘 2 큰술, 다진 생강 2 작은술

준비 과정

1 양념 재료는 한데 섞어둡니다.

2 오징어는 껍질과 뼈를 제거한 후 물기를 없애고 5cm 길이에 0.5cm 폭으로 썰어 오징어 액젓에 3시간 정도 재둡니다.

3 무는 0.5cm 두께에 5cm 길이로 잘라서 소금을 살짝 뿌려 30분 동안 절여둡니다.

4 오징어와 무를 한데 섞어 양념으로 버무린 후 병에 담고 5~7일 후에 먹기 시작합니다.

Spicy Oysters

어리굴젓

6~8 Servings

2 lb.	Oysters, removed from shells

Seasoning

6 Tbsp	Dried red pepper powder
4 Tbsp	Salted anchovy sauce
1 clove	Ginger, julienned very thin
2 oz.	Garlic, julienned very thin
1 tsp	Sugar
1 Tbsp	Sesame seeds
1/4 cups	Scallions, chopped

Preparation

1 Combine seasoning ingredients in a medium-sized bowl.

2 Rinse oysters in salt water. Combine oysters with seasoning ingredients and place in a jar. Refrigerate for 2~3 days before serving.

3 Serve garnished with sesame seeds and scallion.

6~8 인분

900 g	굴
6 큰술	고춧가루
4 큰술	멸치액젓
1 쪽분	가늘게 채 썬 생강
50 g	가늘게 채 썬 마늘
1 작은술	설탕
1 큰술	참깨
1/4 컵	다진 파

준비 과정

1 양념 재료는 한데 섞어둡니다.

2 소금물에 굴을 씻어 물기를 뺀 후 양념에 버무려 줍니다. 유리병에 담아 냉장고에 2~3일 정도 보관한 후 바로 먹습니다.

3 상에 내기 직전 참깨와 파를 넣고 버무립니다.

Seasoned Spinach · Bean Sprouts Cucumbers 시금치나물, 콩나물 무침, 오이나물

4 Servings

Seasoned Spinach

8 oz.	Spinach, uncooked

Seasoning

1/4 tsp	Garlic, minced
1 Tbsp	Scallion, chopped
1 tsp	Sesame oil
2 tsp	Sesame seeds
TT*	Salt

Seasoned Bean Sprouts

8 oz.	Bean sprouts

Seasoning

1/4 tsp	Garlic, minced
2 Tbsp	Scallion, chopped
2 tsp	Sesame oil
1 Tbsp	Sesame seeds
1/4 tsp	Salt

Seasoned Cucumber

4	Kirby cucumbers
1 tsp	Salt
As needed	Vegetable oil

Seasoning

1 tsp	Garlic, minced
1 Tbsp	Scallion, chopped
TT*	Salt, sesame seeds

Preparation

Seasoned Spinach

1 Bring a pot of water to a boil with a pinch of salt. Blanch spinach for approximately 1 minute and squeeze out excess water.

2 Combine spinach with seasoning ingredients. Serve immediately.

Seasoned Bean Sprouts

1 Bring water and a pinch of salt to a boil in a medium-sized pot over high heat. Add bean sprouts and cook covered for about 10 minutes. Remove sprouts and drain.

2 Add sprouts to seasoning ingredients and toss well. Serve garnished with sesame seeds.

Seasoned Cucumber

1 Wash cucumbers in salt water. Cut cucumbers crosswise into 1/8-inch slices and season with 1 teaspoon of salt. Let sit for at least 10 minutes. Rinse and squeeze to remove excess liquid.

2 Heat vegetable oil in a medium-sized pan over medium heat and sauté minced garlic and cucumber for 5 minutes. Take off heat and add scallion and salt to taste. Serve garnished with sesame seeds.

4 인분

시금치 나물

225 g	시금치 한 단

양념

다진 마늘 1/4 작은술, 다진 파 1 큰술, 참기름 1 작은술, 참깨 2 작은술, 소금 적당량

콩나물 무침

225 g	콩나물

양념

다진 마늘 1/4 작은술, 다진 파 2 큰술, 참기름 2 작은술, 참깨 1 큰술, 소금 1/4 작은술

오이 나물

4 개	오이
1 작은술	소금
적당량	식용유

양념

다진 마늘 1 작은술, 다진 파 1 큰술, 소금 · 참깨 적당량

준비 과정

시금치나물

1 뜨거운 물에 소금을 넣고 끓으면 깨끗이 씻은 시금치를 넣고 살짝 데친 후 차거운 물에 헹궈. 물기를 꼭 짜둡니다.

2 시금치에 양념을 넣고 손으로 가볍게 무쳐서 바로 상에 냅니다.

콩나물 무침

1 중간 크기 냄비에 물을 붓고 약간의 소금을 넣은 후 끓입니다. 끓으면 콩나물을 넣고 10분 정도 뚜껑을 덮고 삶아냅니다. 익으면 건져 체에 밭쳐둡니다.

2 콩나물에 양념을 넣고 손으로 가볍게 무칩니다. 깨를 살짝 뿌려 접시에 담아냅니다.

오이나물

1 소금으로 오이를 깨끗이 씻어 양끝은 잘라내고 0.3cm 정도로 얇고 동그랗게 썰어 소금 1작은술에 10분 정도 재둡니다. 물에 한 번 씻은 후 물기를 꼭 짜둡니다.

2 중불 프라이팬에 식용유를 두르고 마늘을 볶다가 오이를 넣고 5분 정도 볶은 후 파, 소금을 넣고 불을 끕니다. 참깨를 뿌려 상에 냅니다.

Koreans do not typically indulge in heavy deserts. Korean meals are usually finished off
with fruit, rice cakes, and tea.

한국 사람들은 후식으로 과일을 주로 먹고, 식혜, 수정과 같은 찬 음료를 후식으로
마시기도 합니다. 떡 종류는 주로 간식용이었으나 요즘은 후식으로 많이 사용된답니다.

Desserts

디저트

Stuffed Rice Cakes · Omija Tea Song Pyun 송편 · 오미자차

Tri-Color Dashik 삼색 다식

Caramel Rice Yak Shik 약식

Sweet Red Bean Rice Cakes 웃지지

Sweet Rice Dumplings Gyung Dan 삼색 경단

Roasted Pineapple with Three Berries 세 가지 베리를 곁들인 구운 파인애플

Black & White Sesame Seed Sticks 깨강정

Steamed Rice Cakes · Cranberry Tea 백설기 · 크랜베리 차

Stuffed Rice Cakes · Omija Tea

Song Pyun 송편 · 오미자차

4 Servings

Stuffed Rice Cakes

1 lb.	Rice powder
5~6 Tbsp	Water, boiling
1/3 cup	Sesame seeds, crushed
1 Tbsp	Honey
2 Tbsp	Sugar
TT*	Salt, sesame oil

Omija Tea

1/2 cup	Omija
3 cups	Water
1/2	Pear
As needed	Pine nuts
TT*	Sugar

*TT : To Taste

Preparation

Stuffed Rice Cakes

1 Combine sesame seeds, honey, and sugar in a small bowl. Set aside

2 Combine rice powder and salt in a large bowl and sift once. Add 5~6 tablespoons of boiling water and knead into a dough.

3 Roll dough out (1/4-inch thick) and cut out circles (3-inch diameter). Place about 1~2 teaspoons of sesame seed mixture in the center and fold over. Seal well by pinching together edges.

4 Place stuffed rice cakes into a bamboo steamer layered with cheesecloth. Steam for 20~25 minutes and rinse with cold water. Blot dry rice cakes and brush with sesame oil.

5 Serve with hot tea.

Omija Tea

1 Boil a pot of water and omija for 20~30 minutes. Remove from heat and let sit for 30 minutes.

2 Serve garnished with pear and pine nuts. Add sugar as needed.

Tip Tea can also be served cold over ice.

---

4 인분

송편

450 g	쌀가루
5~6 큰술	끓인 물
1/3 컵	부순 참깨
1 큰술	꿀
2 큰술	설탕
적당량	소금, 참기름

오미자차

1/2 컵	오미자
3 컵	물
1/2 개	배
적당량	잣, 설탕

준비 과정

송편

1 작은 볼에 참깨와 설탕, 꿀을 섞어 소를 준비합니다.

2 쌀가루에 소금 간을 해서 중간 체에 거른 후 끓인 물 5~6큰술을 쌀가루에 넣고 많이 치대면서 익반죽합니다.

3 반죽을 밤알만한 크기로 잘라 둥글게 빚어 가운데를 오목하게 판 다음, 만들어 놓은 소 1~2작은술을 넣고 잘 아물려서 송편을 빚습니다.

4 찜통에 젖은 면보자기를 깔고 송편이 서로 닿지 않게 안쳐서 20~25분 정도 쪄냅니다. 쪄낸 송편을 찬물에 씻어서 건져내어 물기를 없앤 후 참기름을 발라줍니다.

5 접시에 담아 뜨거운 차와 함께 상에 냅니다..

오미자차

1 오미자에 물을 붓고 20~30분 끓여 오미자 물이 우러나면 불을 끄고 30분 정도 둡니다.

2 예쁜 커피잔이나 머그잔에 오미자차를 담고 꽃모양으로 찍어낸 배와 잣을 띄워 상에 냅니다. 설탕은 기호에 따라 넣어 드시면 됩니다.

Tip 여름에는 오미자차를 식혀서 배 대신 복숭아를 얼음과 함께 띄워 화채로 만들어 드시면 좋습니다.

Tri-Color Dashik

삼색 다식

4~6 Servings

1/2 cup	Bean powder
2 Tbsp	Corn syrup
1/2 cup	Pine flower powder
2 Tbsp	Honey
1/2 cup	Black sesame powder
1 Tbsp	Corn syrup
As needed	Olive oil

Preparation

1 Combine bean powder and corn syrup in a small bowl. Set aside.

2 Combine pine flower powder and honey in a small bowl. Set aside.

3 Combine sesame powder with 1 tablespoon of corn syrup in a small bowl and steam over a pot of boiling water for 20 minutes.

4 Brush a dashik mold lightly with olive oil and place 3 different mixtures into the mold.

5 Remove and serve with tea or coffee.

Tip Chocolate or cocoa powder can be substituted for bean, pine flower, or black sesame powders.

4~6 인분

1/2 컵	콩가루
2 큰술	시럽
1/2 컵	송화가루
2 큰술	꿀
1/2 컵	흑임자가루
1 큰술	시럽
적당량	올리브오일

준비 과정

1 콩가루를 시럽 2큰술에 섞어 둡니다.

2 송화가루도 꿀 2큰술에 섞어 준비합니다.

3 흑임자가루와 시럽 1큰술을 섞어서 사기 그릇에 담아 찜통에 넣고 20분 정도 쪄낸 다음(기름이 많아 기름을 없애기 위함) 조그만 절구에 쪄서 기름이 빠지게 합니다.

4 다식판에 올리브오일을 살짝 바르고 밤톨만큼씩 떼어서 다식판에 박아냅니다.

5 세 가지 색을 예쁘게 배열하여 그릇에 담아냅니다.

Tip 초콜릿 가루나 코코아 가루를 사용하여 다식을 만들어도 좋습니다.

Caramel Rice Yak Shik
약식

4~6 Servings

3 cups	Sweet rice
2 Tbsp	Caramel syrup
1/2 cup	Brown sugar
2 Tbsp	Sesame oil
1 tsp	Cinnamon powder
2 Tbsp	Soy sauce
3 Tbsp	Raisins
5	Chestnuts, peeled, chopped
TT*	Honey, cinnamon powder, sesame oil, pine nuts

*TT : To Taste

Preparation

1 Soak 3 cups of sweet rice in water overnight.

2 Combine rice with caramel syrup in a large bowl. Steam rice mixture in a steamer lined with cheesecloth for about 1 hour.

3 Combine rice, brown sugar, sesame oil, cinnamon powder, and soy sauce in a large bowl. Fold in raisins and chestnuts and let sit for 1 hour.

4 Steam mixture in a steamer lined with cheesecloth for another 30~40 minutes. Remove, let cool, and cut into shapes using cookie cutter.

Tip Add more brown sugar if caramel syrup is unavailable.

4~6 인분

3컵	찹쌀
2 큰술	캐러멜 시럽
1/2 컵	흑설탕
2 큰술	참기름
1 작은술	계피가루
2 큰술	간장
3 큰술	건포도
5 개	잘게 썬 깐 밤
적당량	꿀, 계피가루, 참기름, 잣

준비 과정

1 찹쌀 3컵을 하루 전날 물에 담가둡니다.

2 불린 찹쌀을 캐러멜 시럽에 버무려 면보를 깐 찜통에 넣고 1시간가량 쌀이 푹 무르게 찝니다.

3 찐 찹쌀은 그릇에 부어 흑설탕을 넣고 밥알이 한 알 한 알 떨어지게 주걱으로 고루 섞어줍니다. 참기름, 계피가루, 간장 순서로 넣어서 맛을 낸 후 건포도와 밤이 부서지지 않도록 잘 섞어줍니다. 간이 배도록 1시간 정도 실온에 둡니다.

4 찜통에 젖은 면보를 다시 깔고 30~40분 정도 더 쪄서 여러 가지 모양의 틀에 찍어 담아냅니다.

Tip 캐러멜 시럽이 없으면 흑설탕을 조금 더 넣어도 됩니다.

Sweet Red Bean Rice Cakes

삼색 웃지지

4~6 Servings

White

1 cup	Sweet rice powder
2~3 Tbsp	Water, boiling

Pink

1 cup	Sweet rice powder
1/2 Tbsp	Cactus powder or pink food coloring
2~3 Tbsp	Water, boiling

Green

1 cup	Sweet rice powder
1/2 Tbsp	Green tea powder
2~3 Tbsp	Water, boiling

Stuffing

2 cans	Red bean paste
2 Tbsp	Cinnamon powder
As needed	Olive oil, parsley, pine nuts

Preparation

1 Combine rice powder with boiling water and knead into dough. Set aside.

2 Combine rice powder and cactus powder with boiling water and knead into dough. Set aside.

3 Combine rice powder and green tea powder with boiling water and knead into dough. Set aside.

4 Combine red bean paste and cinnamon powder in a medium-sized bowl. Set aside.

5 Roll out the three types of dough, cut into 2-inch pieces, and form each piece into flat ovals.

6 Heat olive oil over low heat in a medium-sized pan. Add dough pieces and cook each side for about two minutes. Remove from heat and let cool.

7 Place one teaspoon of stuffing in the center of each piece of dough. Fold dough over and seal, covering the stuffing completely.

8 Serve garnished with parsley and pine nuts.

4~6 인분

흰색 웃지지

1 컵	찹쌀가루
2~3 큰술	끓는 물

분홍색 웃지지

1 컵	찹쌀가루
1/2 큰술	백년초 가루나 식용색소
2~3 큰술	끓는 물

녹색 웃지지

1 컵	찹쌀가루
1/2 큰술	녹차가루
2~3 큰술	끓는 물

소

팥앙금 2 캔, 계피가루 2 큰술

적당량	올리브오일, 파슬리, 잣

준비 과정

1 찹쌀가루에 끓는 물을 섞어 익반죽하여 흰색 반죽을 만듭니다.

2 찹쌀가루와 백년초 가루를 섞은 후 끓는 물을 넣어 익반죽하여 분홍색 반죽을 만듭니다.

3 찹쌀가루와 녹차가루를 섞은 후 끓는 물을 넣어 익반죽하여 녹색 반죽을 만듭니다.

4 팥앙금과 계피가루를 섞어 안에 넣을 소를 만듭니다.

5 세 가지 색깔의 찹쌀 반죽을 각각 손으로 밀어 길게 만든 후 5cm 정도로 잘라 타원형 모양으로 도톰하게 빚어줍니다.

6 프라이팬에 올리브오일을 두르고 약한 불에 천천히 눌러서 모양을 만들어가며 2분 정도씩 양쪽을 지져냅니다.

7 익혀낸 떡에 팥앙금을 한 수저씩 넣고 팥이 다 덮이도록 양쪽을 여며서 모양을 만듭니다.

8 파슬리와 잣으로 모양을 내 접시에 담아 차와 함께 상에 냅니다.

Sweet Rice Dumplings Gyung Dan

삼색 경단

4~6 Servings

6 cups	Sweet rice powder
3 Tbsp	Water
1/2 cup	Black sesame seed powder
1 Tbsp	Sugar
1/2 cup	Mung bean powder
1 Tbsp	Sugar
1/2 cup	Cinnamon powder

Preparation

1 Combine sesame seed powder and sugar in a bowl. Set aside.

2 Combine mung bean powder and sugar in a small bowl. Set aside.

3 Combine sweet rice powder and water in a medium-sized bowl. Line a bamboo steamer with cheesecloth and steam rice powder mixture for about 20 minutes.

4 Remove and knead rice mixture over until dough is formed. Spread dough on a cutting board brushed with salt water into a 1-inch thick layer. Cut dough into 1-inch pieces and roll into balls.

5 Coat rice balls in one of the three powders and serve.

4~6 인분

6컵	찹쌀가루
3큰술	물
1/2 컵	흑임자가루
1 큰술	설탕
1/2 컵	녹두가루
1 큰술	설탕
1/2 컵	떡 계피가루

준비 과정

1 작은 볼에 흑임자가루와 설탕 1큰술을 섞어둡니다.

2 작은 볼에 녹두가루와 설탕 1큰술을 섞어둡니다.

3 중간 볼에 찹쌀가루와 물을 부어 잘 섞은 후 찜통에 면보를 깔고 20분 정도 쪄냅니다.

4 쪄낸 떡을 절구에 넣고 찧은 후 꺼내서 도마에 소금물을 바르고 떡을 쏟아냅니다. 이것을 2.5cm 굵기로 펴서 길게 만든 후 다시 2.5cm 간격으로 고르게 썰어 동글동글하게 모양을 빚습니다.

5 동글게 만든 떡 위에 흑임자가루, 녹두가루, 계피가루 믹스를 묻혀서 경단을 만듭니다.

Tip 카스텔라 가루를 체에 내리면 카스텔라 경단이 되어 아이들에게 맛있는 간식거리가 됩니다.

Roasted Pineapple with Three Berries
세 가지 베리를 곁들인 구운 파인애플

4 Servings

1 tsp	Vanilla extract
2 Tbsp	Triple sec
2 Tbsp	Amaretto
2 Tbsp	Water
2 Tbsp	Brown sugar
1	Large pineapple
2 Tbsp	Cinnamon powder
1 stick	Butter
1/2 cup	Blueberries
1/2 cup	Blackberries
1/2 cup	Raspberries

Preparation

1 Combine vanilla extract, triple sec, amaretto, water, and 1 tablespoon of brown sugar in a small bowl. Set aside.

2 Peel pineapple and sprinkle with cinnamon powder.

3 Melt butter in large pan over medium heat and add 1 tablespoon of brown sugar. Add whole pineapple and cook for 4~5 minutes, rotating the pinapple so all sides cook evenly.

4 Place pineapple on a baking pan covered with foil. Pour vanilla mixture over the pineapple. Bake in a 400°F oven for about 40 minutes or until caramelized. Rotate the pineapple while baking so all sides cook evenly.

5 Remove the pineapple from the oven and cut into 1/2-inch thick slices. Arrange berries over pineapple and serve immediately.

Tip Orange juice can be substituted for triple sec.

4 인분

1 작은술	바닐라 향료
2 큰술	트리플 섹
2 큰술	아마레토
2 큰술	물
2 큰술	흑설탕
1 개	파인애플
2 큰술	계피가루
100 g	버터
1/2 컵	블루베리
1/2 컵	블랙베리
1/2 컵	라즈베리

준비 과정

1 작은 볼에 바닐라 향료, 트리플 섹, 아마레토, 물 그리고 흑설탕 1큰술을 섞어 놓습니다.

2 파인애플 껍질을 잘라 파인애플 전체에 계피가루를 뿌려둡니다.

3 프라이팬에 버터를 녹이고 나머지 흑설탕을 넣은 후 완전히 설탕이 녹으면 파인애플을 굴려 가며 4~5분 정도 지져냅니다.

4 오븐 팬에 파인애플을 옮겨 담고, 준비된 바닐라 믹스를 부어서 파인애플이 부드럽게 캐러멜 화될 때까지 200℃로 예열된 오븐에 40분 정도 구워냅니다. 구울 동안 밑에 있는 주스를 뿌려 주거나 파인애플을 돌려가며 방향을 바꿔 골고루 구워지게 해줍니다.

5 팬에서 파인애플을 꺼낸 후 1cm 두께로 잘라 접시에 담고, 블루베리, 블랙베리, 라즈베리를 골고루 뿌려 상에 냅니다

Tip 트리플 섹 대신 오렌지주스를 사용할 수 있습니다.

Black & White Sesame Seed Sticks

깨강정

6~8 Servings

Syrup

1/2 cup	Honey
2 Tbsp	Corn syrup
2 Tbsp	Water
TT*	Salt

Black Sesame Seeds and Walnuts

1 cup	Black sesame seeds
1/2 cup	Walnuts, chopped

White Sesame Seeds and Pumpkin Seeds

1 cup	White sesame seeds
1/2 cup	Pumpkin seeds
As needed	Olive oil

*TT : To Taste

Preparation

1 Combine honey, corn syrup, water, and a pinch of salt in a small bowl. Cook over a double boiler until mixture reaches a thick consistency. Set aside.

2 Cover a square mold with plastic wrap and lightly brush with olive oil. Set aside.

3 Rinse black sesame seeds and roast in a medium-sized pan over medium heat for 7~10 minutes. Reduce heat to low and add chopped walnuts and 3 tablespoons of syrup. Mix well for about 5 minutes. While the mixture is still warm and viscous, pour over the square mold and spread out evenly. Cut into sticks before mixture cools.

4 Brush shapes with remaining syrup and serve garnished with dried dates or pine nuts.

5 Repeat with the white sesame and pumpkin seeds.

6~8 인분

시럽

1/2 컵	꿀
2 큰술	물엿이나 시럽
2 큰술	물
적당량	소금

호두를 넣은 검은깨 강정

1 컵	검은깨
1/2 컵	굵게 다진 호두

호박씨를 넣은 흰깨 강정

1 컵	흰깨
1/2 컵	호박씨
적당량	올리브오일

준비 과정

1 작은 볼에 분량의 꿀과 물엿, 물, 소금을 넣고 섞은 후 중탕을 해 깨강정에 섞을 시럽을 준비합니다.

2 사각 틀이나 그릇에 랩을 깔고 올리브오일을 살짝 발라 준비합니다.

3 검은깨를 잘 씻어 프라이팬에 넣고 7~10분 정도 볶다 호두를 넣고 볶습니다. 그 후 만들어 놓은 시럽 3큰술을 넣고 5분 정도 잘 섞어줍니다. 한 덩어리로 뭉쳐지는 듯하면 식기 전에 준비된 사각 틀에 재료를 붓고 밀대로 얇고 평평하게 펴줍니다.

4 깨가 완전히 식어서 딱딱해지기 전에 2.5cm 두께의 막대 모양이나 아니면 다른 원하는 모양으로 잘라줍니다. 시럽을 위에 발라 대추나 잣으로 장식해도 좋습니다.

5 흰깨와 호박씨를 섞은 흰깨 강정도 같은 방법으로 합니다.

Steamed Rice Cakes · Cranberry Tea

백설기 · 크랜베리 차

Steamed Rice Cake

8 cups	Non-glutinous rice powder
7~10 Tbsp	Water
1 cup	Sugar

Cranberry Tea

1 lb.	Cranberries
1	Orange
1	Lemon
3/4 cup	Red wine
1/2 cup	Honey
TT*	Honey

Vinegar Water

2 cup	Water
1/4 cup	Vinegar

* TT : To Taste

Steamed Rice Cakes

1 Sprinkle water on rice powder and sift once. Combine powder with sugar in a large bowl.

2 Layer a bamboo steamer with cheesecloth and cooking spray. Sprinkle sifted rice powder evenly into the steamer and steam for 30 minutes. Remove from heat and let sit covered for another 10 minutes. Rice cake is done when it produces no powder when poked.

3 Slice and serve with coffee or tea.

Tip Kidney beans or raisins can be added to the rice cake mixture before steaming.

Cranberry Tea

1 Wash cranberries, orange, and lemon. Soak in vinegar water for 15 minutes and rinse. Cut orange and lemon into pieces without removing the peels.

2 Blend cranberries, orange, lemon, wine, and honey in a blender until smooth. Place mixture in a jar and store in refrigerator.

3 Add 1~2 tablespoons of the fruit blend to a cup of hot water and honey. Stir well and serve.

백설기

8 컵	멥쌀가루
7~10 큰술	물
1 컵	설탕

크랜베리

450 g	크랜베리
1 개	오렌지
1 개	레몬
3/4 컵	레드와인
1/2 컵	꿀
적당량	꿀

식촛물

물 2컵, 식초 1/4 컵

백설기

1 멥쌀가루에 물을 뿌려서 손으로 비벼서 중간 체에 내린 후 설탕을 고루 섞습니다. 손으로 뭉쳐서 살짝 올려 던져봐서 부스러지지 않을 정도의 수분 상태가 되어야 합니다.

2 대나무 찜통에 면보를 깔고 스프레이 오일을 뿌려준 후 쌀가루를 살살 안칩니다. 이때 누르면 절대로 안 됩니다. 냄비에 물이 끓으면 대나무 찜통에 뚜껑을 덮어 30분 정도 찐 후 약한 불에 10분 정도 뜸을 들입니다. 꼬치로 찔러봐서 하얀 가루가 묻어나지 않으면 완성된 것입니다. 하얀 가루가 묻어나면 군데 군데 찔러서 스팀이 통과하게 하여 더 익힙니다.

3 접시에 담고 커피나 차와 함께 상에 냅니다.

Tip 쑥을 섞어 만들 수도 있고, 콩을 삶아 섞을 수도 있고, 건포도를 넣어 건포도 설기를 만들 수도 있습니다.

크랜베리 차

1 크랜베리, 오렌지, 레몬을 깨끗이 여러 번 씻은 후 식촛물에 15분 정도 담가 두었다가 꺼내 씻습니다. 오렌지와 레몬은 껍질까지 같이 잘게 썰어둡니다.

2 크랜베리, 오렌지, 레몬, 레드와인, 꿀을 블렌더에 갈아 병에 넣고 냉장고에 보관합니다.

3 뜨거운 물에 크랜베리 믹스 1~2큰술과 꿀을 적당히 타 잘 저어서 상에 냅니다.

Beef Stock
쇠고기 육수

2 lb.	Beef, flank or brisket
16 cups	Water
1/2 lb.	Korean radish, peeled
1	Yellow onion, peeled
15 cloves	Garlic, peeled
1	Large green onion

Preparation

1 Soak beef in water for 30 minutes. Remove and rinse.

2 Place beef in a large pot with enough water to cover and bring to a boil. Remove beef and rinse pot.

3 Add beef back into the pot along with the radish, onion, garlic, large green onion, and 16 cups of water. Bring to a boil, reduce heat to low, and let simmer covered for 1 hour. Skim surface residue from stock.

4 Discard garlic and large green onion. Remove beef and set aside. Let stock cool for about 2 hours or until it reaches room temperature. Discard radish and onion.

5 Pour stock into containers and store in freezer.

6 Add 1 cup of water to every 4 cups of stock when making soups or stews.

1 kg	사태나 양지머리 쇠고기
16 컵	물
230 g	껍질 벗긴 무
1 개	껍질 벗긴 양파
15 쪽	마늘
1 개	대파

준비과정

1 양지머리는 30분 정도 물에 담가 핏물을 뺍니다.

2 냄비에 고기가 덮일 만큼 물을 붓고 한소끔 끓으면 고기는 건져내고 냄비는 깨끗이 씻어줍니다.

3 깨끗이 씻은 냄비에 양지머리, 무, 양파, 마늘, 대파와 물 16 컵을 넣고 끓기 시작하면 뚜껑을 닫고 중불로 1시간 정도 끓입니다. 중간에 찌꺼기나 지방을 걷어줍니다.

4 마늘과 대파는 버리고 무와 양파는 그대로 둡니다. 그래야 식히는 동안 무와 양파에서 물이 나와 국물 맛이 좋습니다. 2시간 정도 식힌 후 무와 양파를 버립니다. 고기는 꺼내 수육으로 먹거나 다른 국을 만들 때 사용합니다.

5 식힌 육수는 통에 담아 냉동실에 얼려두었다가 필요할 때 꺼내서 쓰면 됩니다.

6 국을 만들 때는 육수 4컵에 물 1컵을 더 넣고 끓여줍니다.

Dried Anchovy Stock

멸치 육수

20 cups	Water
12 oz.	Radish, peeled
1	Yellow onion, peeled
10 or 6	Dried shitake mushrooms
10 cloves	Garlic, peeled
1 oz.	Ginger, peeled
1 oz.	Dried kelp
4 oz.	Dried anchovy
1	Large green onion

Preparation

1 Bring 20 cups of water, radish, onion, dried shitake mushrooms, garlic, and ginger to a boil in a large pot. Reduce heat to low and simmer for 40 minutes.

2 Add kelp, anchovies, and large green onion and simmer for another 20 minutes.

3 Remove from heat and let stock cool for 1 hour. Strain stock, pour into containers, and store in freezer. Add 1 cup of water to every 4 cups of stock when making soups or stews.

20 컵	물
170 g	껍질 벗긴 무
1 개	껍질 벗긴 양파
10개	마른 표고버섯
10 쪽	마늘
30 g	손가락 길이의 생강
15 g	마른 다시마
60 g	마른 멸치
1 개	대파

준비과정

1 물 20 컵에 무, 양파, 마른 표고버섯, 마늘, 생강을 넣고 끓기 시작하면 중불로 40분간 끓여줍니다.

2 다시마, 멸치, 대파를 넣고 20분간 끓입니다.

3 불을 끄고 1시간 정도 식힌 후 내용물을 건져내고 통에 담아 냉동실에 얼려두었다가 필요할 때마다 녹여서 사용합니다. 국이나 찌개를 끓일 때는 멸치 육수 4컵에 물을 1컵 정도 더 넣어 사용하면 됩니다.

Glossary of Cooking Techniques

Al Dente (알 덴테)

A firm (but not hard) texture. Noodles cooked to al dente should retain some bite.

Blanch (데치기)

To immerse in boiling water for a few minutes and then immediately dip into an ice water bath for a brief moment

Deep fry (튀김 방법)

When deep frying, remove ingredients from the fryer half-way through cooking. Let cool on paper towel for a few minutes and return to the fryer to complete cooking. This results in a crisper fry.

De-vein (새우 내장 제거하기)

The "vein" of a shrimp is its digestive tract. To de-vein shrimp, gently score a shrimp with a paring knife to expose the vein. Grab a hold of one end of the vein and gently pull it out.

Egg omelet (달걀지단)

To make an egg omelet, whisk eggs in a bowl and pour into a pan over medium-low heat. Flip over (do not fold) when one side has finished cooking and continue cooking until the second side has cooked through.

Egg wash (달걀물)

To make an egg wash, whisk eggs in a bowl until uniform in consistency and color.

Julienne (채 썰기)

To cut into long, thin slices

Steamed rice (밥 짓는 방법)

If a rice cooker is unavailable, add 1 cup of water for every cup of rice to a pot. Bring to a boil, stirring occasionally. Reduce heat to low and let simmer covered for 20 minutes. Turn off heat and let sit for another 10 minutes covered.

Glossary of Cooking Terms

Asian pear (아시아 배)

Sweeter and juicier than American pears, Asian pears can be found in most Asian markets.

Bean powder (콩가루)

Available in Korean markets (ask for "kong karu")

Belt fish (갈치)

A flavorful fish available in Korean and Japanese markets (ask for "gal chi")

Black bean sauce (블랙빈 소스)

Earthy and rich, black bean sauce can be found in most Asian and many American markets.

Black sesame powder (검은깨 가루)

This nutty powder can be found in Korean markets

Black sesame seeds (검은깨)

Available in Korean markets

Burdock root (우엉)

A crisp, sweet root available in most Asian markets

Cactus powder (백년초)

Used primarily for food coloring, cactus powder can be found in Korean markets

Chili sauce (칠리소스)
Available in most Asian and some American markets under the name Sambal Oelek

Crab sticks (게살)
Available in most Asian and American markets

Crown daisies (쑥갓)
A slightly bitter green, crown daisies can be found in Asian markets (in Korean markets, ask for "sukgat")

Curry cake (고형 카레)
A mild Japanese style solid curry available in Korean and Japanese markets

Curry powder (카레가루)
A mild Japanese style curry powder available in Korean and Japanese markets

Dashik mold (다식 틀)
Dashik molds are available in most Asian markets. Any small cookie or petit four mold can be substituted for dashik molds

Dried kelp (다시마)
Harder and thicker than dried seaweed, dried kelp is available in Korean markets (ask for "dashima")

Dried thin noodles (소면)
Available in Korean markets (ask for "Somyun")

Dried thick noodles (칼국수 면)
Available in Korean markets (ask for "kal gooksoo")

Dried seaweed (마른 김)
Available in Korean and Japanese markets

Dried small anchovies (잔 멸치)
Available in Korean and Japanese markets

Dried red pepper powder (고춧가루)
Available in Korean markets (ask for "kochu karu")

Enoki mushrooms (팽이버섯)
Available in Asian and some American markets

Fish sauce (피시소스)
A salty, fermented South Asian sauce available in Asian and many American markets

Fried bean curd pockets (유부)
Available in Korean markets (ask for "yubu")

Green tea powder (녹차가루)
Available in most Asian and American markets

Goma shabu sauce (미소 샤브 소스)
A miso-based shabu sauce available in Korean and Japanese markets

Hichimi (히치미)
A spicy Japanese seasoning available in Korean and Japanese markets

Jelly fish (해파리)
Available in Korean markets (ask for "haepari")

Jeon (전)
A Korean style pancake made with a variety of meats, seafood, and vegetables

Jorangyi rice cake (조랭이 떡)
Available in some Korean markets (regular rice cakes can be substituted for jorangyi rice cakes)

Jumbo gyoza wrappers (만두피)
Thick, round Japanese dumpling wrappers available in Asian and some American markets

Glossary of Cooking Terms

Kimbop (김밥)

A Korean style maki

Kimchi (김치)

A spicy Napa cabbage preparation available in Korean and some Asian markets (ripe kimchi has been fermented for a few days in a refrigerator)

Korean buckwheat noodles (냉면)

Available in the refrigerator section of Korean markets (ask for "naengmyun"). Keep refrigerated until ready to use.

Korean chives (부추)

Available in Korean markets (ask for "buchu")

Korean corn syrup (물엿)

Thicker than American corn syrup, Korean corn syrup is available in Korean markets

Korean mustard (한국 겨자)

Spicier than its American counter-part, Korean mustard paste is available in Korean markets

Korean radish (한국 무)

Available in Korean and Asian markets

Korean watercress (미나리)

Available in Korean markets (ask for "minari")

Korean yam (한국 고구마)

Sweeter than American yams, Korean yam is available in Korean and Japanese markets (ask for "goguma")

LA beef short rib (LA갈비)

Beef short ribs cut to include three rib bones; available in Korean markets (ask for "LA kalbi")

La yu (라유)

A Chinese chili sauce available in Asian markets

Large green onion (대파)

An Asian scallion available in Asian markets (in Korean markets, ask for "daepah")

Mirin (맛술)

A Japanese cooking wine available in Korean and Japanese markets

Miso (일본 된장)

A Japanese fermented soybean paste available in Korean and Japanese markets

Montreal seasoning (몬트리얼 시즈닝)

A meat seasoning available in American markets

Mung beans (녹두)

Available in Asian markets (ask for "nokdu")

Mung bean jelly (청포묵)

A solid, tofu-like cake made from Mung bean available in Korean markets (ask for "chungpo muk")

Mung bean powder (녹두가루)

Available in Korean markets

Mung bean sprouts (숙주)

Available in Asian and some American markets

Non-glutinous rice powder (멥쌀)

Available in Korean markets

Omija (오미자)

A flavorful Asian berry available in Korean markets

Orange supreme (오렌지 수프림)

Slices of orange without the peel or membrane

Oyster sauce (굴소스)

A thick, earthy sauce available in Asian and most American markets

Panko (빵가루)

Japanese style breadcrumbs available in Japanese and Korean markets (ask for "bang karu" in Korean markets)

Pickled radish (쌈 무)

Available in Korean markets (ask for "ssam moo")

Pine flower powder (송화 가루)

Available in Korean markets (ask for "songhwa karu")

Pollack fish roe (동태알)

A salty fish roe available in Korean and some Japanese markets (ask for "dong tae al")

Pon shabu sauce (간장 샤브 소스)

A soy-based shabu sauce available in Japanese markets

Red bean paste (팥앙금)

A sweet bean paste available in Korean markets (ask for "pot angum")

Red pepper oil (고추기름)

Available in Korean markets

Red pepper paste (고추장)

A sweet, spicy paste available in Korean markets (ask for "kochujang")

Rice cake (떡국 떡)

Available in Korean markets (ask for "dukgook duk")

Rice powder (쌀가루)

Available in Korean markets (ask for "ssal karu")

Roasted black bean sauce (자장 소스)

A rich sauce available in Korean markets (ask for "jajang")

Salted anchovy sauce (멸치액젓)

A salty anchovy-based sauce available in Korean markets (ask for "myulchi eckjut")

Sesame leaves (깻잎)

A pungent leaf available in Asian markets (ask for "ggenip")

Soybean paste (된장)

A Korean fermented soybean paste available in Korean markets (ask for "dwen jang")

Spring mix salad (샐러드 믹스)

A mix of young salad greens that can be found in most American markets

Spring roll wrappers (라이스 페이퍼)

Thin, semi-transparent wrappers available in Asian and many American markets

Squid sauce (오징어 액젓)

A salty sauce available in Korean markets (ask for "ojinguh ekjut")

Sweet potato starch noodles (당면)

A Korean noodle similar to vermicelli (ask for "dahng myun")

Sweet rice (찹쌀)

Available in Korean markets (ask for "chap ssal")

Sweet rice powder (찹쌀가루)

Available in Korean markets (ask for "chap ssal karu")

Tempura batter mix (튀김가루)

Available in Asian and many American markets

Vinegar powder (식초가루)

Available in Korean and Japanese markets

Wasabi paste (와사비)

A Japanese root paste similar to horseradish available in Asian and many American markets

White sesame seeds (흰깨)

Available in Asian markets

Wonton wrappers (완탕피)

Thin, square dumpling wrappers available in Asian and many American markets

Congratulations

Good food is such an important part of our heritage and culture.
Your Cookbook will be added to our collection of favorite items from our wonderful trip to Seoul, Korea. We look forward to exploring your Korean recipes!
Congratulations on your culinary arts!
Sincerely,

Rotary Club of Chicago President (2005–2006), Robert and Evy Alsaker

Dear Soyearn,
I was so pleased to hear that are writing a cookbook that should be of great value to anyone interested in Korean cuisine. Our Chicago community has such wonderful connections to other cultures. Our vibrant Korean American community in addition to the many visitors we host will find your book fascinating.
Congratulations,

Rotary Club of Chicago President (2008–2009), Arol Augsburger, O.D.

To be perfectly honest, I have never cooked Korean food and only until recently did I ever eat at a Korean restaurant. So an expert on Korean cuisine and Korean recipes, I am not.
But I can tell you that great cooking, as well great books, starts with passion, and my good friend and fellow Rotarian Soyearn Yoo has put her heart and soul into this wonderful book. I have spent much of the past year listening to her plans for writing this book and I was honored that she asked me for this contribution to her finished product.
Her book is beautifully photographed, easy to follow, and I am sure that all readers, Rotarians and non-Rotarians alike, will enjoy tasting her authentic recipes.

Rotary Club of Chicago, Editor–in–Chief, The Rotarian Magazine, Vince Aversano

Congratulations to Soyearn Yoo, a student of mine at Kendall College, for putting all her effort and knowledge into Korean Kitchen. This book is more than just a collection of recipes - it highlights her family's traditional recipes as well as her personal heritage. Soyearn has also managed to update the recipes into an easy and understandable format for the home chef.

Culinary Adjunct Coordinator, Michel Coatrieux

Congratulations to Ms. Soyearn Yoo on her cookbook. As a former English teacher in Ansan, Korea, I can truly appreciate a cookbook from someone with Soyearn's expertise! I met Soyearn when she became a member of the Rotary Club of Chicago, the world's first Rotary Club. I have been continually impressed with her dedication to the Chicago and international communities through her volunteer service. I am positive that this cookbook will be helpful to the underserved children of the world and a great tool for cooks around the world!

Rotary Club of Chicago President (2006~2007)/ Don Garner

Several years ago, a fellow Rotarian, Ms. Soyearn Yoo, told me that she planned to publish a Korean cookbook in time for the 2009 Rotary International Convention. Subsequently, Soyearn started taking courses at the Culinary Institute of Kendall College in Chicago. She even went so far as to travel to Korea to take courses on traditional Korean cuisine.

Ms. Yoo is well known in the Korean community here in the Midwest for her frequent articles on Korean cooking and is often called the "Korean Julia Child". Julia Child became famous for her TV cooking program and cookbooks. Ms. Yoo is also becoming famous in her own right. She is generous in offering her services as a cook and instructor for many worthwhile charities.

I myself am exceedingly glad that Soyearn Yoo is now sharing recipes for traditional and nouveau Korean dishes with people throughout the world via her new cookbook.

Congratulations!

Rotary Club of Chicago/Former Fannie Mae Vice President, Andy Kim

Congratulations on this wonderful cookbook and the tasty recipes it contains! Food in any tradition is more than just the ingredients, it contains; it is a powerful method of communicating kind thoughts from its preparer to those who enjoy its presentation, flavors, textures, and aromas. May the recipes in this book that you prepare for your friends and family be enjoyed in that spirit.

Rotary Club of Chicago President (2009–2010), Angelo J. Loumbas

I would like to extend my heartiest congratulations to Ms. Soyearn Yoo on the publication of this cookbook after having researched and studied Korean cuisine for a number of years.

For those that may not know, Ms. Yoo has been faithfully serving the church she attends, as well as the Korean community in Chicago. As a member of the Rotary Club of Chicago, she has also been involved in various service related activities, both locally and internationally.

Also in line with her desire to serve, Ms. Yoo holds a special place in her heart for the needy and underserved children. It is her ardent desire to help these children through the publication of this cookbook. I have complete confidence that this book will not only be cherished among the Korean community and throughout the world, but will ultimately bring great benefit to those beloved children.

Rotary Club of Chicago/MCOH Corporation President, Michael H. Oh

Soyearn was an outstanding student and always committed to excellence.
She always exceeded my expectations, and always did her best. She is one of the rare students who make teaching a joy. As her culinary instructor at Kendall College, I hope I have provided a bit of inspiration for Soyearn to write her cookbook. Congratulations!

Pierre Pollin

Congratulations on the completion of your cook book! I am happy to hear about the progress towards completing your dream of publishing a cookbook.
As president of the word's first Rotary club, I found that people will give their time and their money to things they have a passion for. The publication of your cook book demonstrates your passion for "Service Above Self".
Once again, congratulations on making your dream real.

Rotary Club of Chicago President (2007-2008), David W. Templin

품격 높은 한국요리의 전승

우리가 살고 있는 미 주류사회에 품격 높은 한국요리를 알리고 우리 후세들에게는 한국요리를 전승시키고자 요리책을 출간하심에 진심으로 축하드린다.
유소연 님은 받으신 은사, 요리솜씨를 수십 년간 갈고 또 닦으셨다. 요리에 대한 열정을 불사르며 계속 배우고 연구하며, 만들고 또 만들고, 장인의 경지를 지나 요리를 예술로까지 승격시킨 요리 예술가이다. 더구나 지난 수십 년간 맛있고 멋있는 요리로 많은 분들을 초대해 대접해 주셨다. 그분의 요리는 보기에도 너무 아름다워 감탄을 하며 즐겼던 기억들이 생생하다. 받은 은사로 사회에 공헌하고 싶어 책 판매 수익을 모두 커뮤니티를 위해서 쓰겠다고 하신다. 유소연 님은 아름다우며, 마음씨가 곱고 생각이 반듯하며, 강인한 의지의 현대 여성상이다. 또한 시카고 한인 여성회 이사님이시기도 하다. 다시 한 번 축하드립니다.

시카고한인여성회 이사장 구광자

전문 요리인으로의 성공 축하

유소연 님을 알고 지낸 지도 거의 20년 가까이 되어간다. 미모에 따뜻한 마음씨가 한결같아서 주위 사람에게 늘 향기를 풍기는 듯하다. 그분은 살아가는 모든 면에 열정을 품고 산다. 신앙생활도, 골프 치는 것도 열심이다. 그 중에 가정을 으뜸으로 여겨 남편과 가족의 밥상을 열심히 차리는 분이다. 이제 그 솜씨로 전문 요리학교(Culinary School)까지 졸업해 전문 요리인으로 성공했다. 그 열정을 이어 여기 훌륭한 책을 출판하게 된 유소연 님께 사랑과 존경을 한껏 보내며, 많은 한인들과 자녀들에게 이 책이 널리 읽혀지기를 바란다.

아시안 휴먼서비스 디렉터 마주해

빼어난 음식문화로 서구 홍보

시카고에서 32년여 동안 교우해 온 유소연 님이 이번에 영문판 한국 요리책을 출간하게 됨을 축하드립니다. 유소연 님은 한인 사회복지를 위한 행사에도 도움을 아끼지 않는 등 동포 사회에 많은 기여를 하고 계신 분이기도 합니다.

음식문화에 있어 우리 선조들은 발효(Fermentation)를 이용하여 된장을 만들며, 특히 채소를 소금에 절여 발효시키는 한국인 특유의 김치를 창안하였던바, 요즈음 한류를 타고서 〈대장금〉 드라마가 지구촌 곳곳에서 인기리에 각광을 받고 있는 이유도 한국 전통음식 문화의 핵심이 바로 '참살이(Wellbeing)'에 바탕을 두고 있기 때문입니다. 음식에 음양의 조화를 맞춰 요리해 보양하려 했던 우리 선조들의 슬기로움이 전 세계적으로 먹거리 사업에도 벤치마킹을 하고 있는 셈이 된 것입니다. 바로 이러한 시기에 격조 높은 한국 전통요리법을 담은 책자가 발간된다는 사실은 한국의 빼어난 음식문화를 우리 후손들에나 서구 사회에 널리 홍보를 한다는 점에서도 그 의미가 사뭇 크다 하겠습니다. 거듭 축하드립니다.

노스이스턴 대학 교수 박규영

음식 나누기 운동, 나눔의 삶 실천

음식문화의 대국인 중국에서도 한국음식 열풍이 불고 있습니다. 북경, 상해, 홍콩 등지의 대형 한국 요식업체들이 늘어나고 있습니다. 그러나 정작 한국음식을 가르칠 수 있는 서적과 음식을 만드는 재료 등의 기준이 많이 없다는 것을 인지하게 되었습니다. 이때 유소연 씨가 한국 음식문화를 알리기 위한 영문판 요리책을 출판하게 되어 참으로 기쁘기 그지없습니다. 유소연 씨는 그리스도의 사랑을 소리 없이 실천해 오신 분입니다. 불우한 이웃을 위해, 교회와 지역사회 봉사를 위해, 전 세계에 소외된 사람들을 위해, 특히 중국에 살아가고 있는 조선족 학생들을 위해, 굶주림으로 고통당하는 북한 주민들을 위해 음식 나누기 운동을 오랫동안 실천해 오셨습니다. 이제 한 발 더 나아가 사랑의 실천으로 한국 음식문화를 세계에 알리는 홍보대사의 역할을 담당하게 되신 유소연 씨의 노고를 높이 치하하며 더 나아가 한국 음식이 각국 여성들로 하여금 식탁에 올려지게 되기를 바랍니다. 축하드립니다.

중국 심양기술고등학교 교장 반호

전문요리책에 큰 기대

유소연 씨는 25년 전 아이들을 키우면서 알게 된 사람입니다. 인생의 한 삶 속에서 아이들의 양육을 위하여 같은 경험을 공유했던 가깝게 지냈던 사람이 요리책을 출간한다 하니 호기심과 더불어 뚜껑을 열어보고 싶어지는 충동을 가지게 됩니다. 나는 요리하고는 거리가 먼 사람이라 요리를 잘하는 사람이 제일 부러운 대상입니다. 자녀를 잘 키우는 분으로만 알고 있다가 전문적으로 요리책을 발간하신다 하니 너무 반갑고 기다려집니다. 자녀를 키우며 갈고 닦은 솜씨로 며느리와 같이 내시는 첫 요리책을 가이드로 삼아 자신만의 요리를 창조할 수 있음에 매우 흥미롭고 기대가 큽니다.

시카고 포스터은행 이사장, 한미 텔레비전 사장 배명화

궁중비법과 퓨전의 창작품

음식은 사람을 행복하게 만든다. 정성을 다해 늘 새롭게 만들고 기쁨으로 먹고 마시면 세상을 향한 온갖 에너지가 솟아난다. 오래전 유소연 씨를 만난 건 초창기의 두레선교회와 봉사단체 등을 통해서였다. 그런데 내가 중앙문화센터 원장으로 있던 어느 날 궁중요리를 배우고 싶어하는 그녀를 다시 만났다. 그때 나는, 그녀가 무엇보다 한식의 세계화에 뜨거운 가슴과 사명감을 가졌음을 알아차렸다. "60이 지나면 재미없을 터이니 되도록 빨리 진정으로 하고 싶었던 일이 있으면 시작하라"고 부추겼을 뿐인데, 얼마가지 않아 그녀는 자신의 꿈을 단계적으로 이뤄내기 시작했다. 며느리 유정화 씨와 함께 중앙일보 시카고 판에 '2대가 함께하는 요리' 연재를 시작한 데 이어, 유명한 요리학교(Culinary School)에 적을 두는가 하면, 어느새 한국의 최고 궁중요리 전문학원에서도 지극정성으로 배우며 음식의 지경을 넓혔다. 시간 속에 소멸되고 사장되고 마는 것이 얼마나 많은가? 그런 것들을 건져 올리는 소연 씨가 너무 예쁘다. 전통의 궁중비법과 퓨전을 넘나들며, 손과 마음으로 창작해낸 이 요리책이 세계 속에서 대를 이어가며 사랑받게 되기를 소망한다.

시인, 시카고 중앙일보 종교전문위원 배미순